The Wise Lesbian Guide to Getting Free from Crazy-Making Relationships and Getting on With Your Life

Amber Ault, Ph.D., MSW

Getting Free from Crazy-Making Relationships

Contents

Getting Free from Crazy-Making Relationships

GRATITUDE

I am deeply indebted to a number of people for their contributions to the development of the project that became this book.

First and foremost, I thank the women who agreed to allow me to interview them for the book. I appreciate your sharing with me the difficult, painful stories of the toxic relationships you survived, the lessons you learned along the way, and the great news of your recovery, resilience, and capacity to move on to happier times and healthier relationships. Your stories will inspire others as they have inspired me.

Several friends and colleagues agreed to be beta readers of the manuscript-in-progress. Their feedback was invaluable, as was their ongoing encouragement to bring this project to fruition for the benefit of readers. I am especially grateful to Betsy McKenna, Carla Corroto, Pat Rodriguez, and Nora Jacobson for conversations about the manuscript and, more importantly, for their steadfast friendship.

Deborah Radel brought a literal sunburst of color into my world in the midst of the dark Solstice days of winter 2012, just as I was beginning to work on this project, became a steady force of friendship and encouragement, and served as a perfect audience for the very first, very rough, draft. Ann Cothran, whose extraordinary grace has always inspired me, kindly read a close-to-done draft and offered professorial encouragement. Colleague Anne Totero read a preliminary draft of the first chapter and offered an invaluable suggestion for its development. Stu Koblentz and Justice Robinson both have provided levity and perspective. Thank you to each of you for your presence in the process of this book's evolution and in my life.

My mother, MaryLou Ault, has always supported my work and my dreams, and has especially encouraged me to write. I am aware every day how a parent's love can be a person's saving grace, and how fortunate I am to be her daughter.

Brian Daly of DNA Music Labs in Madison, Wisconsin, recorded and edited the audio version of the book. In addition to his technical acumen, he brought to the project an attentive ear that assisted me in re-writes and a genial spirit that made the recording process a pleasure.

The likelihood that this book would have taken any shape at all without Julie Tallard Johnson's skillful writing coaching seems very, very small. I think of Julie as a book doula, and her combination of skill and experience as a coach and editor on the writerly side of things and as a clinician on the conceptual side were a perfect match for the development of this project. This book is not my first, but with Julie's coaching and support, this is the project that has, at long last, crystallized a piece of my identity as a writer. For all of that magic, I am grateful.

I am very fortunate to have had access to excellent clinical training around personality disorders and trauma-informed care, which is so often valuable in working with partners of people with personality disorders. Dr. James McGloin, my amazing colleagues at the Emergency Services Unit of JMHC, and Professor Dave LeCount at the University of Wisconsin-Madison School of Social Work all have specialized training in trauma and personality issues, and I consider myself deeply fortunate to have had access to the rich learning environments they've created. I am especially grateful to Dr. McGloin for his careful reading of the penultimate draft of this manuscript and for his ongoing clinical supervision and support.

This book has a practical orientation and a theoretical foundation that I trace to the fortunate, formative period in my first round of graduate training in anthropology and sociology, when I had the great luck to be hired by Sue Green, then the coordinator of the Rape Education and Prevention Program at Ohio State University. There, I served as a rape prevention educator and self defense instructor. During my years working as a REPP consultant, Sue nurtured the evolution of my thinking and interests around violence against women, growing as it did to encompass the gendered aspects of anti-gay hate crimes and, ultimately, intimate violence within LGBTQ communities. With Sue's support, Gloria McCauley, founder of the Buckeye Region Anti-Violence Organization, and I developed and taught one of the country's first LGBT self-defense courses. This, in turn, led to our growing recognition, thanks to the students who came and shared their stories, of violence and emotional abuse within same-sex relationships. This book, written two decades later and on the heels of my clinical training in social work, is deeply rooted in what I learned at REPP. I hope it will be a contribution to the projects of creating a peaceful and just world and of improving women's lives, consistent with the work of the feminist writers, thinkers, and everyday activists who came before us.

Getting Free from Crazy-Making Relationships

To Sue Green:

Visionary/

Pragmatist/

Magician/

Scientist/

Revolutionary/

Friend.

Getting Free from Crazy-Making Relationships

INTRODUCTION

I've written this little book with the hope of providing help, support, encouragement, and relief to women suffering in relationships with women partners whose behavior is confusing, difficult, erratic, and exhausting.

A number of wonderful writers have offered excellent recent books about the difficulties that partners experience in relationships with narcissists, sociopaths, and people with Borderline Personality Disorder. Although many authors acknowledge that both straight people and LGBT people experience rollercoaster relationships, few devote explicit attention to exploring toxic same-sex relationships. The groundbreaking books that do focus on the topic of lesbian battering are very valuable to women who are experiencing partner violence, but many women in toxic relationships don't consider their relationships violent, so haven't been drawn to the texts on lesbian battering. Not seeing themselves reflected clearly in either the lesbian battering literature or the general literature on toxic relationships, lesbian partners in crazy-making relationships often spend a great deal of time and money trying to figure out what could explain their girlfriends' erratic, exploitive behavior --- and how to return stability to relationships in which they are "walking on eggshells."

This book offers lesbians a way of understanding the dynamics of toxic relationships that is rooted in the psychology of personality disorders and informed by cultural insights on lesbian culture and the situation of lesbians and other queer women in societies that still exclude LGBT people from full social participation.

How does living in a heterosexist and homophobic society affect your vulnerability to getting involved with a woman who is a narcissist, a psychopath, or a person with Borderline Personality Disorder? How does lesbian culture make it challenging for women like you to get help or to exit a toxic relationship once you recognize that your partner is not who you thought she was when you fell in love with her? This book takes a lesbian-specific look at our vulnerabilities to such relationships, their dynamics, and the barriers LGBTQ people face in getting help, as well as a host of strategies for protecting yourself and recovering from the trauma that partners often experience from such relationships.

I hope you will find my descriptions of three personality disorder patterns that cause a great deal of relationship suffering useful for making sense of the toxic relationship in which you find yourself. Still, this is only one way of thinking about your partner's crazy-making behavior. The important thing for our purposes in this book is not whether your partner has a personality disorder or carries a personality disorder diagnosis in the mental health system, but whether the experience you are having in your relationship supports your well-being, happiness, and capacity to be your best self. You deserve not to suffer in a love relationship, and you have the ability to have a life in which you are not constantly on edge because of your partner's problems, unpredictability, volatility, or manipulations.

This book is designed to help you interpret the toxic dynamic you are experiencing in your relationship and to help you cultivate skills that will allow you to move on to a happier, healthier, more peaceful phase in your relationship life. You deserve to feel loved, valued, and significant in your relationship. If your dream is to be in a relationship, you deserve for that relationship to be full of delight, support, comfort, compassion, and respect. As same-sex marriage becomes legal in more and more places in the world, it is perhaps more important than ever that we choose our partners consciously and carefully, and build our skills in identifying and understanding toxic relationships and how to respond to them.

Our lives are short; our world needs us to be present, engaged, and involved. We can learn much from toxic relationships, it's true; perhaps their most important lesson is that relationships worth having support us in being our best selves and doing our best work for the well-being of the world. We prepare for such relationships with everything that comes before them, including our negative and painful experiences. If you are in or recovering from a toxic relationship now, you can use its lessons as fertile compost for growing a happy life moving forward. I hope this book will be an important tool on your path toward a richly satisfying, deeply rewarding life free of toxic relationships.

Thank you for picking up this book. Now, let's take the first step together.

DESPERATION

Vibrant, healthy, connected relationships support our ability to thrive. Difficult, toxic, and exploitative relationships undermine our health, our happiness, and our ability to bring our best selves to the project of creating a better world. Because same-sex relationships exist in a broader social context that is generally toxic for women and especially invalidating for lesbians, our relationships with each other need to serve as places of rejuvenation and safety, support and inspiration, delight, and joy. Despite a feminist vision of same-sex relationships as offering women intimacy in the context of equality, too many women in same-sex relationships find themselves manipulated, exploited, abused, undermined, and exhausted by the intimate partners they trust to serve as sources of sweetness, security, and comfort.

This book is written for lesbians and other queer women who find themselves in the throes of truly toxic relationships. I've designed it to help you understand toxic lesbian relationship dynamics from multiple perspectives, to support you in overcoming any denial you carry about how deeply devastating a toxic relationship might be for you, to offer you an introduction to the social and personal factors that may have made you vulnerable to a relationship that harms your well-being, and to encourage you to remove yourself from a situation that only waters the seeds of fear, frustration, hopelessness, and exhaustion in you.

In preparation for this book for lesbians about relationships with girlfriends who have the traits associated with narcissistic, sociopathic, and borderline personality disorders, I asked lesbians who had experienced toxic, roller coaster relationships to tell me their stories. Many came forward and graciously agreed to share their experiences, despite the pain sometimes involved in recounting them. All relationships have challenges, but toxic relationships are different from ordinary relationships because the pattern of interaction between the people involved is the fundamental source of misery and confusion in the relationship.

In ordinary relationships, partners may disagree about how to spend money or where to vacation, but disagreements are resolved, hurt feelings are repaired, and the backdrop for daily interactions is respect, kindness, and mutual support. In toxic relationships, problems don't have such clear definitions, and they rarely result in clear, amicable resolutions, because at least one partner lacks many of the fundamentals necessary to functional relationships: the capacity to form attachments to a primary partner; a commitment to integrity, trustworthiness, honesty, and respect; the ability to keep agreements and tell the truth; the capacity to self-soothe and stay centered; the capacity to feel empathy; the ability to modulate our speech; the ability to relate to others genuinely and without exploitation; the capacity to evaluate our own behavior and modify it; the ability to make amends; an openness to influence from our partners; the ability to prioritize our partners' interests over our own when circumstances require; and the ability to tolerate and respond to life's ups and downs without becoming a human roller coaster. Ordinary relationships have conflicts, difficulties, and challenges. In toxic, tumultuous, dramatic, and crazy relationships, relationship dynamics themselves are the problem.

All of the women who talked with me about toxic lesbian relationships have been in other partnerships; all of them had been in relationships with significant longevity, and all of them expressed rational, reasonable expectations about the roles of conflict, reciprocity, and compromise in ordinary relationships. They come from a range of ethnic backgrounds, with a variety of educational credentials and professional histories, and from across the lesbian gender spectrum --- some identify as butch, some as androgynous, some as femme, and some as genderqueer. Almost all have had relatively stable employment. Most own their own homes. Some have been parents. And all expressed dismay, confusion, exasperation, and despair at how their usual strategies and skills for resolving conflict, creating intimacy, and engaging in mutual influence and reciprocal support did not work in the relationships they entered into with toxic partners.

Whether or not they have been diagnosed officially, most of those especially toxic partners have the signs and "symptoms" of one or more of the dysfunctional emotional patterns called "personality disorders." The key common element among personality disorders is difficulty in cultivating and maintaining healthy, mutually satisfying, stable, non-exploitive relationships. Ultimately, lesbians who become involved with personality-disordered women stand little chance of developing healthy partnerships with them, no matter how strong their own relationship skills may be, as the examples I will share in this book illustrate.

Annie, for example, repeatedly exhausted herself in efforts to make sense of her girlfriend's behavior. She took extreme measures, such as allowing her girlfriend, Janelle, to move in with her even though the relationship was clearly unstable. She hoped that living together would soothe Janelle, and decrease her jealousy, tantrums, and erratic behavior. The fact that Janelle is French offered her hope that the behavior she found so confusing could be interpreted through the lens of cultural difference, rather than as personal pathology. When I interviewed her for this book, she said:

I had never been involved with someone from another country. You don't know if that's what it is. I had never met anybody like this before.

I always kept thinking that it was going to change. I kept thinking that it would get better. I kept thinking it had to...you know, as we got to know each other, as she got more comfortable, as she got --- you know she was still kind of new to this lifestyle really --- I thought that if she moved in she would feel more secure and then maybe she wouldn't be so jealous or (reactive) to all that weird stuff that used to just kind of set her off.

Unfortunately for Annie, allowing her girlfriend to move into her home proved disastrous. Instead of stabilizing the relationship, it simply increased Annie's exposure to traumatizing emotional toxicity in the forms of brutalizing, mindless speech and disrespectful behavior:

When she starts her thing, there is no governor on her. There's no thing in her that tells her she's got to be careful of what she says. She just says whatever is coming into her head and there is no governor. So she says all of this horrible stuff to me. It's like having razor blades ripping me up, cutting me up, souffléing me. And I am supposed to stand here with this shield on me and not feel anything. If I say anything to her, even If I just say, "You're hurting me," that slices and dices her as much as anything she is saying to me. So she has no capacity to hear anything, anything negative, but she has no governor about anything she says.

I started not trusting her. She was, like, going through my stuff. I put a lock on my file cabinet because she had been going through my stuff looking for evidence that I'm...what?...bad or something. I had a backpack that I carry back and forth to work. I started putting anything important in there and keeping it by my bedside. I started getting afraid.

18

I had started barring the bedroom door because I didn't know if she would come in. I couldn't sleep all the way because I knew I was afraid she would come in. And I wasn't afraid she was going to do anything to me physically. She's never, ever done that. There was just something about her presence that...I didn't want her coming in and trying to start something. I think that's why I would lock the door or bar the door. I didn't want to be afraid that she was going to come in and try to start a verbal altercation.

When I asked her to move out, it had been nine months and it was just torture for months. She was either in the other room or constantly fighting. I'm having friends telling me I could stay at their house because it was so horrible I didn't even feel comfortable in my own home.

Desperately trying to make her relationship work, Annie had allowed her girlfriend to move in. Nine months later, desperately trying to save her own emotional well-being, she asked her girlfriend to move out. For months after they stopped living together, however, Annie continued to see Janelle --- and to search for some kind of way to understand Janelle's volatility, her ability to "go from 0 to 60 to ballistic" and then to behave "as though nothing had happened," her inability to take responsibility for her own behavior.

Annie is not alone. Other women have been equally desperate for answers and for relief. Bonnie, for example, told me that her need for peaceful respite from her toxic live-in girlfriend became so great that Bonnie would say she had to leave home for a professional conference, drive to a city three hours away, and then check into a hotel to sleep for a few days. She learned that her girlfriend, suspicious, jealous, and controlling, would call the hotel, instead of simply calling her cell phone, to obtain confirmation that she was where she reported. Amanda would work overtime in order to avoid going home to predictably crazy and stressful fights that she says she "couldn't wrap [her] head around, because they weren't ever really about any definable issue" and to avoid the profound sadness of feeling estranged and alienated in her own home. Indeed, none of these women is alone in her suffering and despair related to a toxic partner, although feeling alone is a common denominator among lesbians who have experienced toxic or roller coaster relationships.

As I write, I imagine where you are as you read, how your story echoes the tiny bits of stories I have just shared here. Maybe you have retreated to the guest room in your own home to find some sense of safety from the unpredictable energy of your volatile partner. Maybe you have fabricated a weekend business conference as an excuse to go to a hotel in another city to recharge from your girlfriend's incessant drama. Maybe you are parked in a car, bracing to go home to a self-centered person who will predictably be unwelcoming, unkind, and unappreciative. Maybe you have the good fortune not to live with your personality-disordered girlfriend, so you have some privacy as you read, looking for something to explain how your life has become so crazy. Even alone, however, you are still on edge about whether she will or won't call, will or won't follow-through, will be calm and kind or chaotic and cruel when next you encounter her. Despite your suffering, you regularly debate whether you should stay in this relationship, given how good things can be when things are good, despite how bad things become when they are bad.

As I write, I can imagine your exhaustion --- along with your worry, shame, and confusion. As I write, I can imagine the feeling of addiction and entrapment, the feeling that you cannot remove yourself from a relationship you know to be draining your life energy. As I write, I can feel the hooks she has sunk into your psyche: "she needs me;" "everyone else has left her, so I need to prove people can be good;" and "she is amazing---I just don't make her happy." I can feel you being tugged by the line of her extra-specialness, her promises to do better, and your insatiable curiosity to "figure it out" so you can fix it. I can feel how you are caught in the trap of these questions: "She said she loved me; how can I get us back to that affectionate place?" "She's great in public, so why is she so harsh with me?" and, eventually, "If she thinks I am so horrible, why won't she just leave?" I recognize the quicksand of "resistance is futile" and "I am in so deep that any escape attempt will result in my complete destruction." I observe how that quicksand prevents you from setting yourself free.

By now, you know that you have given more than you actually can afford in terms of money, time, and energy to a woman who somehow never refills your energetic tank or meets your emotional needs. Maybe you have moved across the country; maybe you have drained your bank account or worked yourself into an illness; maybe you have allowed her to set up camp in your home; maybe you have taken in her kids or bailed her out of jail. You have done these things trying to make her life better, thinking that "help" is a hallmark of love or the price of admission to a few more moments in the spotlight of this "remarkable" woman's amazing attention. Because of the depth of your investment already, you may feel hopeless about walking away.

You may stay because you feel trapped. You may stay because you feel obligated, given how responsible you have become for this woman's support, care, feeding, or housing. You may worry about what it would mean *about you* if you walked away; you may also worry about what the consequences could be *for you*, given how unpredictable your girlfriend is. She may threaten that she will kill herself; by alternative, she may threaten to destroy you --- or your reputation, or your custody of your children, or something else dear to you. If you have legal or financial involvements with her, you may be concerned that getting out could cost you your home, financial security, or career. *If you aren't worried about pay-back or fall-out as much as you are about who will take care of her and her vulnerabilities if you leave, you should be.* You are the person about whom I am concerned. The toxic girlfriend will almost always make sure her own needs are met.

If you have worked up the courage to leave, or if you are "taking a break," you may be holding your breath waiting for the other shoe to drop --- especially if you have been through this before. If your toxic girlfriend has borderline traits, you are probably waiting for one of you to re-initiate the dance of "come here-go away." If she is narcissistic or sociopathic, the dance may resume when you apologize to her *for her mistreatment of you* and ask her to give you another chance; she may have convinced you that she is so important to you that being involved with her is worth the price of looking the other way when she lies to you or manipulates you. By alternative, she may toy with you by sending you a letter apologizing (for nothing specific), or simply start texting you again to see if you will accept her overture, thinking that with the passage of enough time, you will forgive her for hurting you without her ever making amends.

For the person with borderline personality disorder, the game centers on abandonment and attachment; for the narcissist, the game turns on adoration, entitlement, and grandiosity; for the sociopath, the game is always about power and sometimes about punishment. For people with any of these personality patterns, the effort to re-unite with you is not about you, but about how hooking you back in benefits them. You perhaps suffer from the illusion that you really aren't seeing what you're seeing or that a person you love would never intentionally exploit, manipulate, or take advantage of you. Until you are confident that you are really done with this relationship, you are still vulnerable.

If you have read this much and feel some resonance between what I am saying and what you are experiencing, chances are that you are in a relationship with a woman who has a personality disorder: sociopathic, narcissistic, or borderline. Chances are also that this relationship won't end well for you, although ending it on your terms as soon as possible will likely be the "most well" thing you can do to create a happy outcome for your life over the long course.

How do I know?

I am a sociologist and psychotherapist. In my clinical practice, in lesbian dating workshops and rollercoaster relationship workshops, and in my preparation for this book, I have worked with and interviewed women who have survived relationships with personality-disordered partners, partners whose personality traits prevent them from having stable, mutually supportive, healthy relationships with others. I have read extensively on these pathologies, and have taken specialty training in providing therapy to people with personality disorders. As a clinician specializing in trauma, I see people in my practice who have been traumatized in relationships with people with personality disorders. As a staff member in a mental health crisis unit, I work with both distressed partners and people with personality disorders, often trauma survivors themselves, whose disordered behavior often frustrates and worries clinicians as much as it does the other people in their lives.

Having worked with personality disordered people, having supported the partners of people with personality disorders as they cope with their relationships or heal from them, and having taken on the task of learning as much as possible through the research literatures on personality disorders, trauma, abusive relationships, and facilitating healthy relationship patterns, I am familiar with many stories of relationship suffering in same-sex relationships, as well as with many stories of recovery from such difficult relationships.

Beyond the experience of supporting others through these relationships, and working with people who have personality disorders, I have had my own direct experience; I know what I know not only as a witness to others' lives but from direct experience in my own. In short, when I work with lesbian partners of women with narcissistic, borderline, and anti-social personality disorders, I can relate to the challenges of both "staying in" and "getting out" --- not only through clinical experience and training , but through familiarity with the territory gained by having lived to tell the tale.

In this book, my goals are 1) to help women like you who are living through the chaotic, dramatic, exploitive, and exhausting dramas of relationships shaped by personality disorders – in particular borderline, narcissistic, and sociopathic personalities --- by mapping out what those disorders are, how they affect relationship functioning, and the consequences they create for partners; 2) to help you look at the factors that may have made you vulnerable to crazy relationships; 3) to aid you in recovering from such relationships by offering practical strategies and useful tools for putting the pieces of your life back together; 4) to help you become more attuned to disordered personality patterns as they show up early in dating relationships so that you can screen future partners more skillfully; and 5) to provide a resource for therapists working with women who are in relationships with personality disordered women partners.

Although this book focuses specifically on women in same-sex relationships, I am confident that much of the material applies to cross-sex relationships as well. The dynamics reported by partners in cross-sex relationships and gay male relationships in which one partner has a personality disorder resonate deeply with women's experiences with women who have personality disorders.

BEYOND LESBIAN DRAMA

One of the hallmarks of personality disorders is that they create problems for the people who have them *and for the people around them.* Women who have entered into relationships with personality disordered girlfriends often find themselves experiencing life difficulties as a result of ongoing drama, stress, financial devastation, legal issues, and the wearing away of their self-esteem and self-confidence. Unlike mental illnesses such as depression, bipolar illness, generalized anxiety disorder, and schizophrenia, which often respond well to medication therapy, personality disorders do not resolve with medication.

To make matters worse, many personality disordered people avoid psychotherapy, especially once a clinician has diagnosed them properly. Personality disorders are often very difficult to treat because personalities --- the stable patterns of how we respond to the world --- are difficult to change. The personality disorders that are most toxic for relationships are those that clinicians identify as Narcissistic, Borderline, and Anti-social Personality Disorders. Below, I give you some flavor of the kinds of difficulties women have faced in toxic relationships with disordered girlfriends. I provide some thumbnail sketches of cases (details, of course, have been changed to protect the privacy of those involved) as a means of helping you determine whether these scenarios have some similarity to the situation you currently face --- and as a means of demonstrating how devastating these relationships can become.

*When Amy– a wealthy dentist---entered the home of Beth without Beth's knowledge, collected her credit card bills, and paid them off three weeks into their dating relationship, Beth, a nurse, interpreted the behavior as a sign of love and generosity. She neither called the police nor immediately ended the relationship. As a result, she signed up for several years of drama that culminated in isolation, physical abuse, and a stress-related illness.

Cathy, a professor from Utah, left a lovely home and a secure teaching position at a prestigious college to take a temporary, one-year appointment at a third-tier school in Vermont because her partner, Doldra, insisted that she would leave Cathy if she wouldn't go. The house Cathy left behind didn't sell, and Cathy faced bankruptcy because she couldn't afford housing costs in two locations --- especially while she was supporting Doldra. Cathy started the tenure-track over, but was fired from her new university because Doldra's drama at home interfered with her productivity. Doldra, who had achieved her goal of moving to Vermont, left Cathy when Cathy's job fell apart, claiming that Cathy's "mental illness" had destroyed their relationship -- despite all of Doldra's "heroic attempts to save the relationship."

* Eleanor, a South Carolina woman on the rebound from a decade-long relationship, put up a Match.com ad a month after her ex-partner moved out. When Frida, an accountant from Portland, Oregon answered and soon claimed to be "head over heels" for her, Eleanor agreed to Frida's proposal to sell her own house and leave her job to relocate to South Carolina. Three months after they began to live together, Eleanor realized that Frida had been neither employed nor owned a home, was not actively looking for work in South Carolina, was a nightmare to live with, and would be very difficult to extricate from her life.

*Gina, a retiree enjoying the good life in Florida, allowed Halle, a much younger, charmingly toxic girlfriend, to move in with her, despite friends' warnings. Within months, Halle quit her job and began draining Gina's retirement funds. Soon, Gina was broke. She had to move from enjoying her retirement in sunny Florida to depending on relatives in snowy Wisconsin, where she sought refuge in her sister's basement. She allowed Halle, who claimed to have nowhere else to go, to come with her.

*Inez, a Wisconsin woman, was shocked to discover that Joyce, whom she had been dating for a year, was still in a partnership with Kris; Inez was stalked by Kris, who believed that Inez was "having an affair" with Joyce. Joyce successfully had convinced both parties for months that each was her "one and only," telling each that the other wouldn't leave her alone, provoking fights with one in order to create space to spend time with the other, and using each for child care for her kids, whom she shuttled between Kris and Inez in order to avoid her own child-care responsibilities.

*Lori, from Indiana, mistook stalking for attentive devotion. She allowed Minna, a disordered partner, to move in with her. Lori suffered property destruction, police involvement, social embarrassment, and legal expenses when she tried to end the relationship. Years later, Minna continued to keep track of Lori's activities and attempted to obstruct any new romance from a distance.

*Pat, an Ohioan, ended her relationship with her long-term, stable girlfriend, Quirisha, when a personality-disordered medical school classmate, Rally, seduced her with promises of marriage and children. Pat was stunned when Rally then dumped her. Rally spent the next two years bouncing back and forth between Pat and another woman. She ultimately married a man --- and continued to have affairs.

*Yielding to pressure to marry as an antidote to relationship struggles, Kate, a Nebraska woman, went to Canada with her disordered girlfriend, Tanya, got married, and dealt with complicated legal consequences as a result. When it was clear that the structure of marriage did not stabilize the relationship, Kate sought a divorce ---- only to discover that she would need to move to a state where same sex marriage is legal or live in Canada for a year to become legally free. Kate and Tanya had purchased property together, and because Kate did not have access to divorce, she could not sell the house and move on without her co-owner's permission. Tanya, of course, refused to agree to sell their home, making exiting very difficult for Kate.

*Ursula, a commercial cruise line captain based on the West coast, allowed Viktoria, her charming new girlfriend from New Zealand, unlimited access to her bank accounts and credit cards while she was at sea for three months. She came home to find her accounts down by half a million dollars.

*A New York social worker, Willy, spent $20,000 on a "honeymoon to Paris" after participating in a commitment ceremony because that was the dream of her girlfriend, Xao-wen. A month after the honeymoon, she discovered Xao-wen had been cheating on her throughout their relationship.

*Yvonne, a Coloradan, made a withdrawal from a retirement account to pay living expenses for her girlfriend, after Zoë expressed desperation about not making enough money at her hourly-wage job to take care of the basics. Yvonne discovered subsequently that Zoë had been buying art books, iDevices, alcohol, and sex toys with money she pretended not to have, and Yvonne's retirement account was subsidizing her indulgences.

*A Georgia massage therapist, Addie, allowed her disordered girlfriend, Beth, to move into her home without paying expenses, even though they had been having ongoing conflict. Addie was concerned about Beth's housing and financial situation and wanted to save her from living in her car, which Beth frequently mentioned, while she "got back on her feet." Once Beth moved in, Addie discovered that Beth would destroy the house if confronted on any issues, essentially making Addie a hostage in her own home.

*A Montana state park employee, Callie, stopped taking anti-depressant medications because her disordered girlfriend, Dee, "didn't believe in" them. Callie returned to drinking after ten years of sobriety because her Dee did believe in drinking. As a result, Callie experienced a resurgence of depressive symptoms and a reduction in her capacity to cope, especially in the face of Dee's unending drama.

*Edie, an Iowa factory worker, lost many hours of her life trying to figure out what she could do to make her relationship with Fiona work. She married Fiona and adopted children with her, thinking this would improve things. Ultimately, Edie needed to remove the children from the home for their psychological and personal safety and dealt with years of legal, emotional, and financial hassle related to child custody.

Do you see yourself or someone you love in some of these scenarios? Reading these examples, it is hard not to wonder how so many smart and decent women could allow themselves to stay in relationships that were clearly exploitive, painful, and damaging. Looking at them from the outside, it is also hard not to wonder if the person being victimized also isn't disordered, although this question runs the risk of victim blame that lets the narcissistic, sociopathic, or borderline disordered girlfriend off the hook. Taken as a whole, these cases may tempt you to wonder whether such toxic relationships are more common than uncommon among women in same-sex relationships. These are all good questions.

Although there is no evidence that personality disorders are more common among lesbians than among women in the general population, I am going to argue that women in queer relationships may be vulnerable to partnering with people with personality disorders for a host of social reasons. I am also going to argue that we need to integrate understandings of personality disordered behavior with our understandings of sexism and heterosexism (see Coleman 1994) to develop a clear interpretation of why so many women have experienced crazy-making levels of emotional toxicity from their partners --- and why they have over-stayed in such unhealthy relationships. Finally, I will argue that if you are presently in this kind of relationship, there is plenty of hope for you to end it, recover, and move on into a life that is free of toxic relationships, toxic girlfriends, and the toxic waste that they inevitably produce. A happy and peaceful place with the prospect of mutually rewarding love with a healthy and kind woman awaits you on the other side of your toxic relationship. In order to get there, let's take this one step at a time.

First, let's talk for a minute about ways of interpreting relationship craziness.

You may not currently think of the volatility in your relationship in terms of domestic violence, or even in terms of abuse. Although your girlfriend may behave in unpredictable, volatile ways, or may lie to you, or may take advantage of your financial generosity, you may not be comfortable with the idea that this is abusive. After all, who wants to see herself as an abused woman? If your girlfriend has never been physically aggressive toward you, her behavior may not conform to your idea of how abusive lovers behave. In this book, we'll re-think this, in an effort to help you interpret what is happening more clearly.

The stereotype of domestic violence, also called intimate partner violence, is certainly heterosexual. From a mainstream feminist perspective, we attribute the dynamics of such relationships to men's cultural dominance over women. It is indisputable that we live in a male dominated society, and indisputable that the systems of that society have protected men who abuse women and children. Nonetheless, there is so much variation in disordered relationships that male dominance alone doesn't completely explain it. Most men in heterosexual partnerships are not abusive. And some women in heterosexual relationships abuse their male partners. What explains the existence of peaceful heterosexual men and straight women who abuse their husbands? What explains abuse in lesbian relationships?

Psychology professor Dr. Ellyn Kashak writes:

Well-accepted analyses of violence based in male-privilege and power may seem irrelevant or inapplicable to lesbians. Yet, while neither partner in a lesbian relationship enjoys male privilege and power, we all live in a society that promotes hierarchy, power differential, inequality, and, yes violence. These are endemic to patriarchy, and why should they not find their way into relationships lived in this milieu? Additionally, lesbian relationships are directly influenced by other societal power inequalities that impact all citizens, including sexism, and those based in class, race, ethnic, and economic inequality, as well as differences in interpersonal power. (2001)

We live in a cultural environment that doesn't promote healthy relationships, and lesbians bear an additional burden of stress based in heterosexism and homophobia,

31

legal and personal discrimination, and anti-gay and lesbian violence. Still, many women in same-sex relationships, like many men and women in heterosexual relationships, do not engage in abusive behavior. Indeed, many are committed to promoting peace and happiness in our households and partnerships. So, in addition to the toxic cultural environment in which our relationships take place, what might further help us understand the characteristics of those who abuse their partners?

Psychologist and psychotherapist Dr. Vallerie Coleman proposed, based on both research and clinical experience, that many women in same-sex relationships who engage in physical or emotional abuse of their partners, like many men with this problem, frequently can be described as meeting the psychological criteria for personality disorders. She emphasized three personality disorders as being especially likely to appear in troubled lesbian relationships: narcissistic personality disorder, borderline personality disorder, and anti-social personality disorder. (People with anti-social personality disorder are popularly called "psychopaths" or "sociopaths.")

My clinical experience and research supports this understanding as a useful way of thinking about the personality characteristics that prove toxic in same-sex relationships among women. This line of thinking doesn't explicitly explain what causes personality disorders --- which may well be linked to all of the forms of oppression that characterize life in capitalist, male-dominated societies --- but it does give us a way to see more clearly the patterns of trouble in particular relationships. As Dr. Coleman notes:

> Historically, many theorists and persons working in the field of domestic violence have been hesitant to acknowledge individual variables as a significant component in battering, for fear that such a perspective would detract from important

sociopolitical factors and serve as an excuse for violent behavior. Rather than negating the importance of social influence, the consideration of individual factors as mediating variables in domestic violence can complement sociological and sociopolitical perspectives. (1994)

Theory works at broad levels of analysis to explain toxic patterns in relationships, but your relationship takes place in your living room, your bedroom, and your psyche, one day at a time. The theories of domestic violence that you know to apply to straight relationships may not allow you to code the suffering you are experiencing in your relationship in terms of "battering" or "domestic violence," yet you know that something in your relationship is very, very wrong. Physical battering is not the only hallmark of toxic relationships. If your girlfriend gives strong evidence of the traits of narcissistic, borderline, or anti-social personality disorder, understanding these disorders will give you new ways to understand what is happening in your relationship and insight on how to move forward for your own sanity and safety.

THE REAL LAVENDER MENACE:

TOXIC GIRLFRIENDS

Are lesbians especially vulnerable to crazy relationships?

Although life has improved in many ways for queer people in recent decades, full social equality, acceptance, and inclusion are far from the reality for LGBT people. Despite pockets of protection and the popularity of *Ellen*, lesbians, bisexual women, and other queer-identified women continue to experience anti-lesbian and gender-based violence, stigma, and discrimination. Like other social minorities, we often maintain public silence about toxic relationships within our communities. We may prefer to keep the details quiet rather than draw attention that reinforces negative stereotypes about crazy lesbians or to avoid further discrimination or violence from law enforcement, the judicial system, and other people who may become aware of abuse, exploitation, or violence within our relationships.

As a result, we often remain unaware of the high rates of abuse in lesbian relationships or dismiss its significance, assuming that it isn't damaging to its victims. We even use the phrases "lesbian drama" and "Grrrl drama" to dismiss pathological behavior between women, as though pathological drama is a normal and predictable element of lesbian life. For lesbians who are not connected to queer communities, or whose relationships are still shrouded in silence, isolation and invisibility make it harder to assess whether toxic girlfriends are simply part of the territory or whether it's appropriate to hold same-sex partners to standards of behavior that would be supported by the general culture.

Despite this public invisibility, social science research consistently tells us that rates of a wide range of verbal, emotional, and physical abuse in women's same-sex relationships equal or exceed the frequency and forms of abuse in heterosexual relationships (Burke & Follingstad 1999; Renzetti 1992; Turrell 2000; Mize & Shackleford 2008). Although research confirms that murder rates in lesbian relationships are far lower than those in heterosexual and gay male couples, studies focusing on abusive behavior document that nearly half of the lesbian couples surveyed acknowledged that at least one partner had used some form of physical aggression during a conflict within the previous year (Coleman 1991; Gardner 1989; & Kelly & Warschafsky 1987, as cited in Coleman 1994); in addition, they reported very high rates of verbal abuse and aggression (Waldner-Hagrud et al, 1997). Although ensuring that lesbian and gay research samples represent the general population is notoriously difficult, and it is possible that the findings reported in these studies are skewed, every study to date that has looked at abuse in lesbian relationships finds patterns of both emotional and physical violence that contradict the stereotype of the conflict-free, cooperative, emotionally literate, egalitarian lesbian relationship.

People across all sexual identity groups have toxic relationships, so lesbians are neither unique nor immune. We may, however, collectively be more vulnerable to cultivating such relationships and we may have greater difficulty exiting them quickly and with ease. The premise of this book is that we should not settle for relationships that are anything less than healthy, happy, and functional. As minority people, we daily face systematic social stress; our relationships with each other need to be places to rest and recharge, places to feel solidarity and ease, places to feel safe, inspired, and welcome. This book is about unpacking what goes wrong in relationships with people who have personality disorders in order to help you move toward relationships that are far more right for you and support you in having what you want and need from life.

Humans are social creatures. We need people, and we need to be needed by others. We are designed to connect, to care, to need care. It is good for our blood pressure, good for our immune system, good for our physical hearts and good for our souls to be in healthy relationships. In contemporary industrialized and post-industrial societies, we live in ways that interfere with this need for connection (Cacioppo 2010). We expect 18 or 22 year olds to be autonomous and self-supporting. "Living independently" is a benchmark of maturity. More of the population of the United States lives alone today than at any other time in any other society in human history. While some of this reflects women's increased autonomy and the social and economic changes that have made solo living viable, it also raises important questions about social disconnection, especially among marginalized groups, like members of the LGBT population. We have designed social systems that work against our own deepest human need to connect. As a result, the stakes for mate selection in general are very high. When lesbians do partner-up, we will turn to those partners, and they to us, to meet a wide range of needs that may exceed the scope of expectations even for cross-sex marriages.

The pull to find a mate, to bond, to partner—and to partner well-- is a deeply human drive. Given all of the roles we expect partners to fill, and how eager we often are to bond, it is not surprising that we can make less than skillful mate choices. People with personality disorders have a penchant for tapping into our deepest needs and desires and, in the early phases of relationships, offering the promise of meeting them. This "talent" taps right into the deep and open longing of women eager to connect. Self-identified sociopath M.E. Thomas, a woman who claims to have exploited and "ruined" several women through their romantic vulnerabilities, says, "People are so hungry for love. They die a little every day for want of it---for want of touch and acceptance....It was so easy....The deeper I went with my love interests, the more they relied on me for their daily happiness, and the drunker I became with power" (2013, p 233).

Becoming more savvy about the capacity of personality-disordered people to give *the appearance of being able to meet one's needs for connection* --- and their difficulty in genuinely following through --- can help you become better at screening out prospective partners whose narcissistic, borderline, or sociopathic traits will ultimately make the intimacy you long for unobtainable. Understanding personality disordered patterns and how they affect relationship functioning will also save you time and energy, and perhaps save you from being further bruised or scarred, while freeing you to make intimate connections with a partner who has more capacity to connect deeply, richly, and with integrity.

Lesbians and other women seeking relationships with women face special challenges in mate selection. Much of this is a matter of numbers, of demographics. We often hear that 10% of any given population is gay or lesbian, but recent research puts the percentage of the lesbian, gay, and bisexual population at 3.5%, with the largest sub-group identifying as bisexual (1.8%), and only 1.7% of the population of the US identifying as gay or lesbian (Gates 2011). That 1.7% is further sub-divided into male and female populations, making the lesbian percentage of the US population less than 1%. That group consists of multiple age cohorts, so that 60 year olds and 16 year olds are all included in that one number; the prospective girlfriends available to 16 year olds and to 60 year olds is then a small fraction of the tiny percentage we began with. Divide any particular woman's dating pool up further by the elements that often result in good matches --- similar educational backgrounds, professional statuses, socioeconomic class, religion, politics, and attractiveness --- and you can see the prospective dating pool for any one woman becoming narrower by the moment. Then, figure in the ways those numbers are further diluted by the vast geographic spaces of this country (match.com and Facebook aside), and the ways homophobia still prevents women from openly identifying themselves as lesbian, and you can see the source of what I call **"lesbian population pressure:"** lesbians' perception that the pool of available partners is so restricted that settling for a toxic or problematic partnership looks like a viable option.

Lesbian population pressure may be further enhanced by the ticking of the clock in any particular woman's life. Social science research documents that more lesbians than heterosexual people or gay men over 50 years of age live alone. Although there is much to be said for independence, autonomy, and going solo (especially when you are exiting a toxic relationship), living alone as we grow into the final decades of our lives can be associated with decreased quality of life, reduced life satisfaction, reduced financial security, and higher mortality.   No wonder, then, that lesbians sometimes lean toward selecting or staying with partners with sociopathic, narcissistic, or borderline traits; given that people with personality disorders can be very charming early in a relationship, that many lesbians recognize the limits of the "dating pool," and that many worry about the specter of aging spinsterhood, we may not screen as long or as carefully as we might --- with disastrous results.

Mate selection may also be more challenging for lesbians because many lesbians don't have much experience or practice with dating (or with dating women) --- again, this is a function of broader cultural and social issues. When many girls are having their first experiences dating boys, many lesbian and otherwise queer adolescents are avoiding dating and trying to survive high school. Even now, despite immense social progress, lesbians often begin to recognize the meaning of our own sexual attraction to girls in environments in which same-sex dating is invalidated or dangerous because of institutionalized homophobia and sexism. If, as adolescents, we have sexual experiences with other girls or become romantic girlfriends, those relationships are often in the closet --- under wraps because of the vulnerability we feel as family members and high school students. As a result, unlike many girls who date boys, we don't have the experience of processing crushes, young love, and budding romances with parents, friends, or classmates. We may not have the experience of moving openly in social settings with our early loves. Because secrecy creates intimacy between those keeping secrets [Richardson 1988], lesbians' early relationships may be insular in ways that prevent us from developing real dating skills, including the skills associated with endings. At the same time, keeping relationships in the closet may reinforce in us the impression that the bonds created by secrecy (similar to adult affairs) define love.

The buffer of privacy surrounding those early relationships offers protection to abusers and abusive behavior. These problems certainly happen in cross-sex relationships, but homophobia, heterosexism, and minority solidarity --- the desire of members of minority groups to not reinforce negative stereotypes of their communities ---- amplifies them in same-sex relationships. Women who come out later, after having dated or having married men, may find themselves similarly at a loss for how to date women in the context of lesbian communities. In both situations --- that of teenagers and that of grown women---women attracted to women face special challenges in cultivating healthy dating relationships---and eventually partnerships---with other women.

RACHEL'S STORY

Rachel & Sarah, for example, found each other in high school and stayed together for several years before finding others with whom to socialize. Eventually, Rachel, who happened to be a minister's daughter, revealed that Sarah had been emotionally and physically abusive with her from the beginning of their very clandestine relationship. Rachel had continued the relationship despite this dynamic. She held felt trapped by the sense that Sarah "couldn't help herself" because she had been abused at home. She accepted Sarah's explanation that she was sometimes emotionally overwrought by the fear that Rachel would leave her---that is, that the abusive behavior was an expression of passionate love and loyalty and fear of loss. Because the relationship was in the closet, Rachel feared risking relationships with family and friends by coming out, especially in a conservative religious environment where anti-gay sentiments were ubiquitous. She worried about destroying Sarah's reputation. She felt a deep sense of loyalty to her first love, as well as a fear of what would happen if she ended the relationship. Finally, she expressed concern that seeking help would reflect badly on lesbians --- a concern that also has some merit, if the only relationships the straight world sees among lesbians are those that require therapy or restraining orders.

\###

Rachel's story reveals how homophobia and heterosexism work as real forces against making great relationship choices in a limited dating pool. Such cultural pressures conspire to keep women in relationships that not only aren't healthy, but are harmful to both the person who is allowed repeatedly to behave abusively and to the person on the receiving end of the abuse. In this case, both young women were missing out on what might be a more positive developmental process, in US culture at least, of dating to determine a good match, learning what feels good and bad in relationships, and acquiring the crucial skill of walking away from toxic relationships. Many women have allowed two assumptions to keep them mired in horrible situations. The first assumption is that current toxic relationship is their only relationship prospect. The second is that being in a toxic and abusive relationship beats being single.

So, are lesbians especially vulnerable to crazy relationships? In a word: *yes*. Are lesbians doomed to be in crazy relationships? Absolutely not.

THE L FACTOR: SOCIAL ORIGINS OF TOXIC GIRLFRIEND VULNERABILITY

Because of lesbian population pressure, heterosexism, and homophobia, the norms that have evolved in lesbian culture over the course of time (the third date moving van scenario actually does happen!), the lesbian dating skill deficit, and what may be unique about the biology of women's sexuality, lesbians have greater vulnerability to getting into crazy-making relationships and more difficulty exiting them. If we lived in a woman-affirming, lesbian friendly, queer-inclusive culture that didn't promote a sense of partner scarcity, relationship invisibility, resignation to dysfunction, and desperation among lesbians, lesbians' ease in choosing appropriate and wonderful partners and cultivating rewarding, loving relationships with them blessed by the support of broad community and family networks would be much greater.

Although most people who end up in toxic relationships do have some special personal vulnerability to these dynamics --- we will talk about this later (see Chapter Four) - -- those personal vulnerabilities are only one element in the equation. The broader social world in which lesbians and lesbian relationships exist contributes to lesbians experiencing toxic relationships. Homophobia and heterosexism work not only to keep LGBT people from full access to the rights and freedoms enjoyed by heterosexual people; they also shape some of the dynamics of our most intimate relationships. Our awareness that law enforcement agencies, battered women's shelters and services, and the legal system that regulates heterosexual marriage and divorce often are not prepared to respond effectively to abuse and exploitation in same-sex relationships (see Mize & Shackleford 2008) also discourages us from seeking help.

Fortunately, despite these challenges, the situation is not hopeless. It is not inevitable that the only women you will have the opportunity to have relationships with are personality disordered. In fact, having seen many women recover from toxic relationships and move on into functional, happy partnerships, I know that quite the opposite is true. The purpose of this book is to support you in creating that possibility for your own life.

If you are currently in a relationship with a woman with a personality disorder, are leaving that relationship, or are recovering from such a relationship, one of your most important tasks is to become both more educated about personality disorders and about your own personal vulnerabilities to them. Doing so means that if you want to date or to be partnered in the future, you may move on to healthier relationships with women who function well, whom you consistently enjoy, who bring out the best in you, and who can support you in having your best life possible. In Chapters 2 & 3, I will offer you a crash course in the most problematic personality disorders for your relationships, and help you perceive personality disordered behavior more quickly and clearly.

NO DYKE DISCOUNT: PAYING THE PRICE OF DISORDERED PARTNERSHIPS

Even healthy relationships have plenty of ups and downs, conflicts, issues, and problems. Relationships where one partner is personality disordered, however, are characterized by extreme behaviors, unpredictability, drama, and various forms of abuse and neglect. In response to the instability introduced into your relationship by your personality-disordered partner, you may find yourself becoming more unstable in your own behavior. You may be making a valiant attempt to restore harmony or equilibrium by placating your disordered partner; you may be too exhausted from responding to a disordered partner's demands, needs, or crises to think clearly, and may make poor decisions as a result. You may lose sight of your good relationship skills and fall into fighting, freezing, or fleeing, only to see things become worse. Whether you are still being conned, in denial, trying to meet your partner's unquenchable and paradoxical needs, or too overwhelmed to make good decisions, you may ultimately undermine your own welfare for a very long time by remaining in a toxic relationship.

To help you understand why it is crucial to be able to identify these patterns and to extricate yourself from relationships that have them as quickly as possible, I offer a list of consequences women have faced as a result of these relationships. My goal here is not to depress or scare you, but to wake you up to the seriousness of the damage that toxic girlfriends can inflict on your life, if you are still in denial about that. What are the negative outcomes for women who have gotten involved with toxic girlfriends?

They:

*have lost jobs

*have lost housing

*have lost property

*have had to file for bankruptcy

*have moved into grandma's basement

*have been stalked

*have been the target of character assassination in their workplaces

*have had to hire attorneys

* have had to file restraining orders

* have had to file in small claims court

*have had exes appear in their homes without permission or notice

*have been physically threatened

*have had houses vandalized, robbed, or burnt down

*have had cars vandalized

*have needed to go into counseling for post-traumatic stress

* have had to request police involvement to stop harassment

* have had to take losses on joint property that must be sold

* have had to pay movers to clear partners' possessions

* have had to change jobs

* have had to heal from affairs and betrayals

* have had to live without access to kids they have parented

* have had to change the locks or install security systems

* have had to move out of state

* have had to file bankruptcy

* have had to deal with major health issues

* have had to address debt and financial loss incurred as a result of the relationship

* have had to reinvent their lives

*have had to deal with leftover issues of trust and trauma as they try to move on into healthier relationships

*have had to deal with isolation and embarrassment related to the shame over being in a toxic relationship

*have lost friends who were worn down from drama fatigue or who wouldn't stand by to watch a friend self-destruct

* have given up pets in order to pacify a disordered partner

*have considered suicide

IT REALLY IS AS BAD AS YOU THINK.

IN FACT, IT MAY BE WORSE

If you are in the midst of experiences like those in the cases presented early in this chapter, you are not alone. Many smart and capable women have been drawn into --- and conned into --- extreme behaviors in the interest of healing, helping, supporting, caring for, pleasing, or appeasing personality disordered partners, and in the hope of ultimately having stable, functional, loving relationships. Indeed, these extreme responses are often a sign of relationships in which personality disordered traits are in play; personality disordered people are often drawn to others who have the capacity to feed their narcissism with "narcissistic supply," to stabilize their borderline dramas with competent problem-solving and endless sympathy, or to buy into their romantic stories of victimization as an explanation for why someone so smart and talented is always in crisis, exploitive of others, or abusive in a variety of ways.

No matter how special you felt as a result of "stepping up" for a disordered partner, at least at the beginning, there are probably a hundred more women that your partner could con into taking care of her in exactly the same ways. If you know much about her history, you may be able to see now that there were several other people she conned before you, or that she is already moving on to her next victim or mark---someone who may soon be seeking this book out in the middle of the night.

To illustrate the idea that women with personality disorders often have a line of women on their "dance cards," and often play these women against each other, here's a description from Bonnie, one of my interviewees, about how her disordered ex-girlfriend, Melinda, could always get her needs met:

> *All the relationships she had, it turns out, started before the last one finished. She would actually have two people living with her at the same time in a couple of instances, and somehow would make each of them believe there was nothing going on with the other.*

Given the devastation to mental health, time, money, reputation, and energy that you can see in the impact list, you can also see that while becoming involved with a narcissist, sociopath, or borderline woman can have its thrills, it often results in financial, practical, social, and emotional devastation. Often, the non-disordered partner will be paying the price for years.

We have started here, rather than with a description of personality disorders, because it is in the pain and confusion and devastation of toxic relationships that partners of narcissists, borderlines, and sociopaths live. If you resonate with the experiences I have described here, chances are you have been involved with a personality disordered partner, and you need help in making sense of your experience, addressing its current realities, recovering from its fall-out, and making a plan for moving forward in ways that help you avoid future relationships that have these patterns. As Annie told me, "I felt like I needed somebody…I was so lost in this thing. I just wanted it to make sense. I needed someone to help me make sense of it. Or tell me that it was messed up."

In the coming chapters, I will help you make sense of the experience of a toxic, crazy-making relationship. You will understand more about personality disorder patterns, what might make you vulnerable to being drawn in by someone with a personality disorder, how to recover from your current situation, and how to screen better and have happier and healthier relationships moving forward.

Getting Free from Crazy-Making Relationships

IT'S HARD TO LIVE THE DREAM IN CRAZY TOWN

We began this book with an overview of the impact of personality disorders on partners, rather than with an overview of personality disorders themselves, because *we can often recognize the presence of personality disorders by the effects the personality disordered person has on others.* Because this is not an academic text but a book for general readers who are in---or are recovering from --- relationships with people with personality disorders, I will put this plain: *a personality disorder is a psychological problem that makes *other people* crazy.* As we noted in the previous chapter, women have taken all manner of extreme actions under the influence of personality disordered partners, and these actions have left them exhausted, financially drained, emotionally devastated, physically ill, socially isolated, suicidal, and sometimes all of the above.

In this chapter, I will help sensitize you to some of the key behaviors of dramatic personality disorders in general, and show you how these disorders cause confusion, frustration, pain, and damage in relationships. If you are still asking whether the trouble in your relationship could stem from a personality disorder, this chapter will help you develop an answer. In the next chapter, we will take a look at the specific features of three personality disorders through a lesbian lens.

IF SHE HAD A PERSONALITY DISORDER WOULDN'T SOMEONE HAVE TREATED IT BY NOW?

Although people with personality disorders sometimes seek counseling, they rarely seek treatment for their personality disorders. Often, because of their intelligence and charm, high-functioning personality disordered people are not recognized as having personality disorders by therapists who aren't particularly astute to personality problems or who prefer instead to think about the problems the person has in different ways, perhaps as attachment disorders, PTSD, ADHD, alcoholism, intermittent explosive disorder, or mood disorder ---all of which may explain some of a particular individual's personality-disordered behaviors.

Unfortunately, therapists sometimes feed into the dysfunctional behavior of the person with many toxic behaviors. For example, sometimes therapists unwittingly praise narcissists for how hard they seem to be working in therapy because they arrive on time, finish homework, and tell entertaining stories. And, of course, the stories that a person with a personality disorder tells about her relationship with you center on how she is your victim, your hero, or your martyr --- and possibly all of the above. In the absence of the full context of actually observing the two of you together in the real world, all a therapist has to go on is a person's limited appearance in her office once a week and her self-report of her own behavior. In the meanwhile, you may wonder why your girlfriend's therapy doesn't improve her functioning in the relationship, feel surprised by your partner's accounts of the therapist's reported praise and affirmation, or be frustrated that your partner is hopping from therapist to therapist without ever gaining any apparent benefit. The benefit to the disordered person, of course, is that you, the partner, may persist in the relationship a bit longer --- precisely because the fact of her being in therapy gives you some hope that things will get better. The following comments represent assessments from partners about why therapy wasn't producing behavioral change in their disordered girlfriends:

She is extremely convincing that she is being wronged. So it always appears that I am this horrible, horrible person. She would go to therapy and tell me things they talked about, and I sounded horrible. The therapist is not getting the real story.

I wasted thousands of dollars on therapy, trying to figure out how we could get on track and live peacefully together, and I might have well used that cash for kindling.

She had a therapist and asked me to go see her with her because we were long-distance and she wanted the therapist to have a sense of me. This was early in the relationship, and there had already been several of these bizarre fights in which she said really horrible, bizarre things to me. I suggested we talk with the therapist about them, but she refused, saying she "wanted to focus on the positive." I respected her wishes, but I realize in retrospect that my exposing her behavior at that point would also have interfered with the image she was trying to maintain with her therapist, who would have been shocked by the details, I think. She did a good job of keeping it together for short periods of time.

When therapists do recognize the presence of a personality disorder and begin to try to address it therapeutically, the client often terminates therapy. Women with Borderline Personality Disorder will complain that the therapist "doesn't understand my problem" and "isn't getting anywhere," while women with narcissistic traits will pronounce the therapist "incompetent" or "not smart enough to work with" them. The therapist who was "extraordinary" and "special" previously is quickly devalued as ineffectual, ill-prepared, and perhaps even damaging, once he or she comes closer to understanding the truth of the disorder from which the client---and the person who loves her --- is suffering. A positive outcome of a therapist recognizing the presence of a personality disorder, even if the person refuses treatment, is that the therapists sometimes warn partners:

> *It helped me to go to a therapist and have the therapist tell me that I was not the crazy one, and I was not going to be --- although Judy was going to paint me in the line of the crazy ones, I was in the line of the non-crazies. That helped. Because I was starting to feel crazy. It had already created physical illness.*

People with personality disorders don't come with official warning labels, and people with a personality disorder diagnosis often choose not to share their diagnoses with prospective partners, although there are exceptions. You need to get hip to the behavioral signs that can substitute for the warning label. Remember, intimate relationship difficulties figure significantly in the profiles of people with personality disorders, and you are in an intimate relationship with someone with this profile.

Do you know that TV show from the 1960's, *Lost in Space*? The show centered on a family, the Robinsons, who were exploring outer space by living on another planet after their ship had crashed. The family had a robot with some anthropomorphic features that made it seem like a member of the family ---- or at least a very loyal and protective pet. Perhaps the most famous line from the show, one that survives to this day in popular culture, came from the robot. In the presence of danger, the robot would flail its arms about, turn its head around, flash its lights on and off, and say in the robotic voice of urgency, "Warning, Will Robinson! Danger! Danger!" Much to my surprise, lesbians often quote Will Robinson's robot to me to express that they saw warning signs at the beginning of a toxic relationship. Several have also quoted the Robinson robot to demonstrate their development of a greater capacity to heed the signals when they now encounter women who have narcissistic, borderline, and sociopathic traits.

The goal of this chapter is to help you develop both a sense of how personality disorders are expressed and a deeper commitment to listening to the "Warning! Danger!" message that your own gut may send you when you experience some of the behaviors associated with these disorders --- even if the woman is charming, even if you have great sexual chemistry with her, even if she pulls at your heart strings, even if she appears to have it all together and whispers sweetly to you about how the two of you can attain everything your heart secretly or not-so-secretly desires. If the warning signs are part of the package, it is important for you to pay attention, whenever they arise, and respond in ways that honor your own welfare.

WHAT ARE PERSONALITY DISORDERS?

Psychology is still a very young science, and the brain, which is intimately involved in behavior, emotion, and perception, is less well understood than any other organ in the human body. In the last hundred years, we have made immense progress in understanding how the brain works, how it is integrated with the mind-body, what it influences and what influences it. We also recognize that we still have only a superficial grasp of this organ and its relationships and interrelationships. As a result, how we think about human behavior, perception, and emotion, what is normal and abnormal, what is healthy and unhealthy, and how to facilitate well-being, build resiliency, and promote and protect recovery from pain, trauma, and abuse, is continually evolving. How Westerners influenced by a European tradition think about these phenomena is also culturally influenced, I should note; what is considered healthy and functional, unhealthy and dysfunctional, and helpful and unhelpful, varies across cultural traditions. So, what I share here derives from a particular cultural context, from the Western practice of psychology, and from the knowledge available at a particular point in time.

Western psychology uses a "disease model" of mental and emotional functioning. In recent decades, activists and scientists together popularized the idea that emotional illness should be thought of as "brain disease." Advocates of this approach argue that viewing emotional problems as reflecting neurochemical imbalances in the brain reduces stigma for patients and for their families, and especially for patients' mothers, who often were held accountable for children's emotional problems --- ranging from psychotic breaks from reality to criminal behavior. The adoption of this perspective has been associated with a shift in training in psychology from a focus on behavior to a focus on neurobiology and neuropsychology, with some important gains in treating mental illness in Western societies.

Within this disease model, mental health practitioners use an institutionalized diagnostic system when they consider how to diagnose and treat people who come into care. This system is described in the *Diagnostic and Statistical Manual 5*, produced by the American Psychiatric Association (2013).

Within this system, psychologists make an important distinction between mental illnesses and personality disorders, with mental illnesses and personality disorders being sorted into two separate categories.

One of the lesbian toxic relationship survivors I interviewed for this book spent hours on-line trying to find a framework within which to understand her disordered girlfriend's erratic, predictably unpredictable behavior. She breathed a sigh of relief when she realized that her girlfriend met the classic criteria for Borderline Personality Disorder:

> *So, I am online and I am googling one day, because I had it in my head that if I could manage the anger part – because that was the thing that was really hard---I thought that if I could just go to an anger management class---for myself---if I could not let her get to me, then I could manage this situation. So I started googling anger or anger mgt, and somehow as I'm googling this there's something that comes up on the side, and it had all these symptoms and it turns out it is Borderline Personality. And I thought "THIS IS IT! I HAVE TOUCHED THE HOLY GRAIL" And I got so excited I called my therapist. "I think I have it figured out! I think I got it. It's this Borderline!" 'Cause I thought that if it was "a thing" it could be fixed. My therapist was like "I think you need to come in to see me." She let me know that this might not be the good news I thought it was.*

Why the excitement? Because Borderline Personality Disorder is not considered a mental illness. That should be good news, right? When the woman above saw her therapist, she explained to her why a personality disorder can be a more damning diagnosis than a mental illness like depression. It makes sense that you might initially be relieved to discover the crazy behavior you have been observing or experiencing is not a mental illness, and that it is a pattern of behavior that is well-documented and even has a name; unfortunately, what appears at first glance to be good news is, in reality, Will Robinson's robot screeching "Warning! Danger!"

Why have Western psychologists decided to construct two basic categories for emotional suffering? Clinicians consider the problems in one category "treatable;" those considered treatment-resistant land in the other category: in the category of personality disorders. The presence of a personality disorder may make the outlook for her, for you, and for your relationship far less optimistic than if her problem were a mental illness. There are some emerging treatments for narcissistic personality, borderline personality, and antisocial (sociopathic) personality disorders, and work in this area continues to evolve. The outlook is better than it used to be, when these patterns of behavior, perception, and emotion were considered all largely untreatable. Even so, the probability that people with these personality patterns will seek effective treatment remains very, very low, and the time they need to spend in treatment is generally very long.

Although there is hope for people with personality disorders to recover when they are motivated to seek effective treatment, my interest in this book is not in exploring the roots of these personality disorders or describing intervention strategies, although these are fascinating areas. Instead, my goal is to address the needs of partners struggling to make sense of the behavior in toxic relationships and to make decisions about how to respond to the confusion, drama, and difficulty that often is rooted in personality disorders.

So, what are the differences between mental illnesses and personality disorders? First, mental illnesses parallel other physical illnesses. Many persons with mental illness probably had a period of functioning well and being emotionally healthy before the symptoms of an illness began.

For example, a person may develop depression after a traumatic loss or prolonged stress; the depression "comes on" and constitutes a change from the person's normal and usual functioning.

Second, mental illnesses are thought to be intimately connected with a person's neurochemistry, and are therefore responsive to medication therapy or to non-pharmaceutical interventions that naturally change brain chemistry. People with depression, for example, may take anti-depressant medication in the form of selective serotonin re-uptake inhibitors (SSRI's) to increase the serotonin, a "feel good" neurotransmitter, available to certain cells in the brain and to alleviate depressive symptoms. By alternative, they may be encouraged to increase exercise, which also promotes the release of hormones that promote feelings of well-being. Either way, the illness is considered connected to biochemical imbalances and treatable through interventions in biochemistry.

Third, and importantly, mental health workers expect that various treatments will decrease symptoms of depression and that the depressive episode will be resolved.

Personality disorders are thought to contrast with these characteristics of mental illness considerably. Clinicians consider personality disorders long-standing – perhaps life-long— patterns of behavior, perception, and responsiveness that interfere with a person's ability to function well, particularly in relationships with others.

Personality disorders are not considered at present to reflect disruptions in neurochemistry, or to be treatable with medications, although there is emerging evidence of structural differences between the brains of personality disordered people and others, so our understanding of this question continues to evolve. Many mental health workers decline to treat people with personality disorders because of the belief that the prospects for effective therapy are low and that the wear and tear on therapists is high. People are not considered to have "episodes" of personality disorders like they have episodes of depression, mania, or psychosis. Personality disorders are consistent; they are on-going, unremitting, and chronic. A person with a personality disorder may "escalate" or have periods in which she is more prone to acting out, but the underlying disorder is always there. When a person with depression becomes very ill, we may be able to hospitalize her and help her re-stabilize; when a person with a personality disorder engages in behaviors that land her in the hospital, her symptoms often become worse.

Personality disorders are not considered, at present, forms of mental illness, even though your experience with a personality disordered girlfriend may have lead you to wonder if she is mentally ill. Unfortunately, the disturbing behavior you have encountered ---the lack of empathy, the inability to take you into account, the manipulation or lying, the come-here-go-away dynamic, the break up/make up cycles, the rages, the inability to accept responsibility for her actions, etc.---is not a function of mental illness as much as it is a function of disordered personality. Indeed, personality disorders give people with mental illnesses a bad reputation.

Mental illnesses don't generally cause people to lie, manipulate, have affairs, exploit others' resources, fabricate facts, or engage in abusive behavior. These kinds of behavior used to be called in common language "character issues." Psychology used to call personality disorders "characterological" problems. You don't need a Ph.D. in psychology to understand what makes up "good character." When one lesbian shared some of the concerns she had about the personality disordered woman she had gotten involved with, her mother responded, "she has bad character." For all of the fancy ways we might think about personality disorders, this simple statement does a good job of summing them up. A partner with "bad character" can cause a host of problems for the woman who falls for her.

TOXIC ELEMENTS

So, let's dig into the kinds of relationship difficulties that often originate with personality disorders. Remember: personality disorders are long-standing patterns of perception, behavior, emotion, and thinking that result in impairments in responding to life circumstances and interpersonal relationships. Caring for someone with schizophrenia or bipolar illness or depression can certainly be exhausting and difficult, but caring for someone with a personality disorder can turn your world upside down, destroy your well-being and self-confidence, and impair your own judgment. It is important to develop a deeper sense of personality disorders if you have been with a disordered partner, so that you can screen more carefully in the future. If you are still involved in a toxic relationship with a personality disordered girlfriend, the sooner you understand the challenges of these disorders, the sooner you will be able to make careful decisions about how to move forward.

The current version of the Diagnostic and Statistical Manual (DSM) published by the American Psychiatric Association (2013) identifies ten different personality disorders. It sub-divides these ten into three groups or clusters, clusters A, B, and C. Cluster A includes three personality disorder patterns ----paranoid, schizotypal, and schizoid. People with these disorders tend to be afraid of, indifferent to, or wary of personal relationships, so chances are low that you would have had an intimate relationship with someone who has any of these patterns. Cluster C includes three disordered personality patterns as well: avoidant, dependent, and obsessive-compulsive personality [not to be confused with obsessive compulsive illness]); these patterns don't usually result in overtly dramatic, manipulative, or exploitive relationship dynamics, although people with these patterns may be highly attractive to narcissists, borderlines, and sociopaths (we will discuss this further in Chapter 3 when we explore what might have made you vulnerable to toxic relationships).

The middle category, Cluster B, includes the four dramatic personality disorders: Histrionic, Borderline, Narcissistic, and Anti-social Personality Disorder (popularly called "sociopathic"). The last three on the list (Borderline, Narcissistic, and Anti-social (sociopathic) are the personality disorders that are most likely to be present in relationships that are crazy-making or devastating for reasonably healthy people.

You will see that there is a great deal of overlap among some of these Cluster B personality disorder descriptions, and to some extent the lines between them are arbitrary. For now, note that commonalities among these "different flavors of crazy," as one of my associates calls them, include the following elements:

1) Deficits in empathy; impaired ability to understand or hold the perspectives of other people
2) Deficits in the ability to care how one's actions affect others
3) Absence of care for others' feelings
4) Deficits in ability to self-sooth
5) Difficulty with emotional regulation ("Flies off the handle; "loses it;" regards yelling and "letting it out" as healthy)
6) Impulsivity and lack of behavioral control (Engages in overspending, over eating, risky sex, over drinking)
7) Distorted sense of self or self-image
    (Estimates her attractiveness, appeal, intelligence, popularity, and achievements more highly than others

do, and has an inflated set of expectations for how others will treat her based on her grandiosity)

8) Comfort with misrepresenting reality and lying (Justifies lying; explains away differences between what she says and what she does or differing accounts of an event at different times)
9) Skill at manipulating others for personal gain or power within relationships
10) Superficial charm and the ability to give the impression of emotional connection
11) "Parasitic" and exploitive lifestyle (Cons others into paying for things on her behalf; lives on others' incomes or uses others' resources; justifies taking advantage of others)
12) Deficits in the ability to take responsibility for their behavior and to experience or express genuine remorse

■■■

In print, this list may seem formal and academic. In reality, these qualities translate into relationship challenges that range from the vexing to the nightmarish. Before we look at the specific traits of borderline, narcissistic, and sociopathic personality disorders in the next chapter, I would like to review some of the common concerns of partners struggling in relationships with personality disordered girlfriends. Just as there is a great deal of overlap between the disorders as psychologists currently think about them, lesbian partners of women with personality disorders also report many common experiences, no matter the diagnosis of their girlfriends (or lack thereof). Here are several common concerns that embody the traits listed above:

■■■

1. Brutalizing speech and disregard for how it affects the partner

Relationships with personality disordered partners often include verbal cruelty, often in the context of "rages," events in which the disordered person's emotional state escalates very quickly into unmodulated rage or jealousy or some other unpleasant feeling state. In this condition, the disordered partner uses demeaning, judgmental, and dramatic language directed at an often unprepared partner, who finds it devastating:

> *It would just seem like she would go from 0 to 60. I mean, it was really quick as to how she escalated and got saying mean stuff like I had never experienced...As soon as she didn't feel like she was the top priority, she would attack me. Looking back now, I realize that she has no ability to self-soothe, to be able to recognize, "this reaction is way more than what is needed." Early on if I would cry, she would call me a martyr and tell me that I was playing her.*

She would just say horrendous things to me. Nobody had ever talked to me like that.

Usually, in the wake of such episodes, the personality disordered woman cannot acknowledge the impact of her cruel speech on her partner; this is one example of the impaired empathy that characterizes these disorders, in greater and lesser degree.

2. Emotional volatility

Many personality-disordered partners exhibit emotional volatility. Sometimes they "go from 0 to 60" when they experience anger or jealousy; sometimes they become volatile when confronted with their own behaviors or when, as is often true for narcissists, their authority is challenged, even accidentally:

We were down at a dance. This friend of hers came up. The friend sits next to me, and chats, and then I actually touched her leg as she was leaving. Janelle saw that, and she started to go ballistic. She was like, "You touched her!" And this jealous thing started to happen. It was just as she was leaving. It was nothing – but- as soon as I did it, I could feel the energy change. She started to get fired up and she stood up like she was going to go leave. And I took her arm, and pulled her down. I said "now, just sit down," 'cause I knew what was coming. And that allowed her to collect herself and that diffused the whole situation. But when we left, I found myself getting mad. And I said to her that I was feeling angry. I am always the one who has to stay in this [even, non-reactive] place. She can be emotional and bounce around and ride the wave, and I always have to be evening her out.

The first time it happened, we had bought a lawn tractor, and we were unloading it in front of my house and she was getting really territorial about how it should be done. She works in the sciences. She's very linear. She just goes off and she starts calling me stupid and stuff like that. And I am like "whoa---that's a really strong reaction for just trying to work together to get the

lawn tractor from the box of my truck. Of course, I am hurt. And I tend to be kinda the beaten dog under the porch. That's my initial reaction. And to wonder what did I do to bring that on?

3. <u>Lying, Manipulation & Gas-lighting (intentionally distorting reality)</u>

An especially crazy-making feature of relationships with women with personality disorders involves distortions of reality --- including understandings about the disordered person's relationship status. The term "gas lighting" refers to a film in which a man endeavors to undermine a woman's faith in her own perceptions by denying her reality and constructing situations to confuse her, with the ultimate goal of convincing her and others that she is insane. Many partners of personality disordered women report feeling gas-lighted as a result of girlfriends leading them to believe in and act according to "information" that ultimately proves to be untrue. For example, many women have started relationships with personality disordered girlfriends with the understanding that the woman was available, only to realize subsequently that other women or men believed that they were exclusively involved with her too. Some lesbians find themselves manipulated out of resources such as housing, money, and labor in response to misrepresentations or conning by disordered girlfriends. These experiences are especially difficult because they can shake the survivor's faith in her own judgment and ability to take care of her own best interests:

> *When we got involved, she told me she was finished with Cat and that Cat had moved to California. Then it came out that they had been "on a break" and that Cat was coming back, but that it was still over and I was still her choice. For a period*

64

of time I saw her less, which she said was because they were spending a lot of time talking about the situation. But then she started talking about how she wasn't sure she wanted to give up that relationship. They had been in it 10 years. It's hard to walk away from something after 10 years. Cat was bringing up some good points. Maybe they could work this out. So this made me redouble my efforts when I should have just walked away. When I would say I was done with the relationship, I would invariably get some sort of phone call that she was coming to my house, extraordinarily drunk, usually at bar time, or that she was going to go out on her motorcycle and drive around and hopefully get into an accident. There were these veiled threats of hurting herself. I would be drawn back in. I didn't want something to happen to her on my account. Then there would be promises about changing.

She said she had cancer. Whether she really did, I don't know. I saw injection marks. She was really sick. I did take care of her. Her hair did thin. I found out later she pulls out her hair. Maybe she is doing heroine? I don't know. I don't know what the truth is. She did have a bunch of pills from the doctor. Then cancer came back. She had cancer years ago and it came back. She would go through periods of not wanting to take the pills. And then she would flush them all and then she never had any money because she would spend it all on pot, I found out. So I don't know what reality is. She called me one day and had me pick her up at the hospital. She couldn't drive. She said she'd had chemo. I said "What about your van?" She said "Oh, we'll get it later." So I never saw it. So I don't know if it was ever really there in the first place. Did the police drop her off for a 72 hour hold? ....I believed her. At the time I believed her. Now I have no idea.

She can keep all of these lies juggling in the air, which makes you think she's not lying because how can anybody remember so many lies and keep them all straight?

There were a lot of things that would happen in our discussions. I thought it was the language thing. Now, I realize it's not the language. She will modify the language to create a different impression. Which can be interpreted as lying. It seems like it's lying. So you don't know if it's lying or if it's this language thing. We'd have these huge discussions. She gets defensive. She never tries to sweet talk you into something; it's always on the defense...which can raise my own defenses.

4. Inability or refusal to accept responsibility or apologize

An important quality of functional relationships is a couple's ability to repair good feelings after some kind of conflict or other event that results in hurt feelings or emotional distance. Personality disordered women often lack the capacity to genuinely apologize, to accept apologies, to make amends, and to set things right:

She could not apologize. Her version of an apology is to say, "You gave me no choice" for some behavior she did. And I was like, "Really?" She did not like being told "when you said this you hurt my feelings." She would say whatever at

night and then get up in the morning like nothing happened.

She couldn't apologize. If I said "it would help if you would say, 'I'm sorry,'" she would say 'I'm sorry,' and then expect whatever it was to be done. It was never organic. These things would happen, and she would tell me we were breaking up, and then she would call like nothing had happen and just pick things up where they left off.

Instead of responding with "I'm sorry" or "I over-reacted," she started lecturing me about "you should have done this instead [so I wouldn't get mad]" and started attacking me. In this line of thinking, my behavior causes her behavior. She never takes accountability for her own behavior.

5. Failure to express appreciation

Lesbian partners of women with personality disorders often make concerted efforts to bring elements of normalcy to the relationship. Indeed, because the disordered girlfriend is so often under-functioning in so many areas, the non-disordered partner begins to over-function. In healthy relationships, a "marital economy of gratitude" operates to create cohesion and reciprocity; in these relationships, efforts to make contributions to express love through acts of caring are often invisible and under-valued. Because the impaired girlfriend cannot genuinely see her partner or her partner's efforts, they cannot be appreciated:

I threw her a birthday party. For a week ahead of time, I had to chip ice out of the driveway because we had had this horrible *storm and I had like eight inches of ice in my driveway. For a week I am chipping ice so people can park in the driveway. I made her lasagna from scratch, I made her a chocolate cake from scratch. I had all this spread, and all night long I had to park people in because the driveway was so narrow. I just busted my ass for a week on this party. And she tells me later, she says that was *the worst* birthday she ever had because I hadn't spent any time with her. I thought ..."Wow." I mean, it just kind of takes your breath away. "What?" But that's her. She just doesn't get it that that was very hurtful. She doesn't get that at all.*

Feeling invisible is a common experience among partners of women with personality disorders. It makes sense, given that impaired empathy and narcissism are common traits among people who have these disorders. Partners often say "it is always all about her," to characterize the perpetual focus on the personality disordered girlfriend's wishes, desires, demands, and issues. In the example above, the birthday girl was unable to recognize the time, effort, planning, and work that her partner had taken on her behalf, leaving her partner feeling unseen, unappreciated, unvalued, and, indeed, criticized for her attempt to create a wonderful experience. If you are having similar experiences in your relationship, pay attention; such examples suggest that the likelihood that you will find validation and appreciation in your relationship is very low.

6. Disrespect and Boundary Violations

People with personality disorders marked by narcissistic, sociopathic, and borderline traits often violate the boundaries of their intimate partners. Forms of violation range from speaking disrespectfully to "snooping" through journals and monitoring text messages, e-mails, calendars and schedules, to violating emotional boundaries, to treating others' property with less care than their own, to stalking, entering ex-lovers' homes, bank accounts, e-mail accounts, and phone records. Many lesbians report that their disordered girlfriends wake them in the middle of the night to fight, so that as time goes on they become more sleep deprived, less resilient, and have greater trouble making good, confident decisions about the relationship.

> We were out somewhere. We came home. As soon as we got in the car to come home, we had this fight. We had been sleeping in separate bedrooms (because) we would have these fights and they were so irrational that at times they were insane. So (this time) I went in my room. I shut the door. I had no sooner shut the door when she opens it and flings in a stack of pictures with a sticky note on top. These pictures had to be gathered before, because this was a very short amount of time. So what she had done was: she had gone through some of my photo albums and she had found some pictures of a girlfriend from 15 years before. And I had never shown these to her. We had had a friend hanging around with us for a day and she had just taken a whole bunch of pictures of us from that one day. We were just hanging around, goofing around, and they were just a nice bunch of pictures. So she had gone through these albums and pulled out these pictures ahead of time, and uses them now, on this opportunity. She throws them on the bed with a sticky note on top of them that says "If you looked at me the way you look at the woman in these pictures, we wouldn't be having these problems." I felt it was so invasive for one thing. And I had never shown them to her because I knew she would probably get jealous because this is the way she is. So, basically, she

went in there and she already had these pulled out that she then tries to use them as an example. She would get so low in the fighting.

One day, I am at work, and I get a phone call from my house (phone) on my cell phone. We work at the same place. She has called in sick, gone up to my house, broken in to my house, and ransacked my house. And (now she) threatens to let my dog out and leave.

She showed up here in a couple of weeks after she moved out. We hadn't talked. She just walked into the house. I have since rekeyed it and everything so that's not an option anymore. She had walked in and it was like 9 am in the morning. There's that gut level response to seeing her. I asked her, "How did you feel when you came into my house without having knocked?" "Nothing. Why?" There's no anxiety or excitement or anything.

7. Emotional Cruelty, Impaired Caregiving, & Sabotage

People with narcissistic, borderline, and sociopathic personality disorders often respond pathologically to situations in which others need to become the center of attention, whether through illness, accomplishment, or a need to focus in order to achieve a life goal. Partners report deep anxiety about these girlfriends' capacity to reciprocate support, provide selfless care, or offer help without using their efforts for their own advantage or self-promotion.

I was stupid. There was one time I was sick. I was so sick that I started getting laryngitis. My throat was getting so bad. And she started picking a fight with me. And she literally would stand in the door, and she's getting us worked up or it's happening. I actually lost my voice for a week and a half. She would stand in the door, or she would walk out of the room and she would fight from a distance, which would make it even worse. But she thinks she took care of me. That's a really bad example. She was horrible. I was sick. She'll tell you about the time I had a kidney stone and I needed a ride to the hospital in the middle of the night and I had to spend a day in the hospital and she came over to my house to feed my dogs and she thinks she's a saint because she did that. And it was all good, but I have done so much for her that she could never compete if there was a list. But she does one thing, and expects [years of recognition]

She was visiting me when her step-father called to say that her mother was in a hospital emergency room having chest pains and breathing issues; the thought was that she was experiencing heart failure. It sounded serious to me. When her step-father asked if she wanted to talk to her mom, she tried to say no and rolled her eyes. When she got off of the phone, the first thing she said was, "Damn it, she always does this to me. Any time I turn my attention away from my mother, she creates some drama designed to suck me back in. I am visiting you, she feels left out, and so she's pretending to have a heart problem." I was really struck by that. She's accusing her mom of pretending to have heart failure---to hijack her attention. Bizarrely, it made her mom's illness somehow *all about my girlfriend* – exactly the thing she was accusing her mom of doing. Her mother truly

71

was very ill. Once she was convinced of that, she went to stay with her for awhile, and her unsuspecting family gave her millions of good-daughter points. All the while she complained to me about being the "childless lesbian" who is expected to always pick up the slack in these kinds of situations, but on Facebook, she had lots of people giving her kudos for being so selfless.

Verbal brutality, manipulation, emotional volatility, boundary violations, lack of appreciation, difficulty with repair and care-giving, and sabotaging behaviors signal the presence of a personality disorder on the part of a partner. When lesbians become involved with partners with personality disorders, their relationships will, by definition, suffer, and so will they. The particular shape of these relationships is influenced by the predominance of some disordered traits over others in the profile of the person with a personality disorder, as well as how you, as the partner, respond to those traits.

THREE VARIATIONS ON THE THEME OF TROUBLE

There are some important distinctions between borderline, narcissistic, and antisocial or sociopathic personality patterns, and those differences have an impact on the dynamics of romantic relationships. They also influence the challenges a lover faces in ending things. Let's take a look at the particular organization of these patterns and dynamics through a lesbian cultural lens here in Chapter Three. We'll explore the features of each of these three disorders and how they play out in relationships.

THE BORDERLINE GIRLFRIEND

There was a little girl, Who had a little curl,
Right in the middle of her forehead.
When she was good, She was very good indeed,
But when she was bad she was horrid.
---Henry Wadsworth Longfellow

We'll start with Borderline Personality Disorder (BPD) for a number of reasons. Clinicians diagnose BPD more frequently in women than in men, so it may be more common than the other personality disorders among women lesbians date. Some of its behaviors map very closely on the classic lesbian "Third Date/U Haul" pattern of overly-quick attachment, in this case followed by a rollercoaster break-up and make-up pattern. The borderline girlfriend can create lots of "lesbian drama"---- for example, affairs, playing one girlfriend against another, break-up threats, retractions of break-up threats, rages, and distortions of reality that make you wonder if you and your girlfriend were in the same conversation.

To meet the full criteria for Borderline Personality Disorder, according to the Diagnostic and Statistical manual 5 (APA 2013) a person only needs to have five of formal criteria for the disorder. I have reformulated the criteria, along with traits I see in clinical practice into the "flashing yellow lights" below. The presence of four criteria might cause you a lot of trouble, but clinically we would only say that a person with only four of these behaviors has 'borderline traits." After I list the signs, I give you a sense of how this personality pattern plays out in everyday life.

SIGNS THAT YOUR GIRLFRIEND HAS BORDERLINE PERSONALITY DISORDER

1. She has a history of on-again, off-again, dramatic romances, possibly with both women and men
2. She exhibits a pattern of changing things up frequently, including friends, girlfriends, religious affiliations, political opinions, career goals, and how she looks
3. She has pattern of emotional volatility

4. She is uncomfortable being single, being alone, and keeping her own company, paired with frantic efforts to prevent herself from being abandoned, even when others do not intend to abandon her
5. She displays an inability to be comfortable in the context of real intimacy
6. She evaluates others as "all good" or "all bad" --- and switches perspectives on the same person quickly and irrationally; vacillating between extremes of feeling, (such as moving from "I hate you" to "I love you" rapidly)
7. She has a history of impulsive behaviors that ultimately undermine her well-being and healthy functioning; these can also undermine yours if you are involved with her. Impulsive spending, binge drinking and eating, and unprotected, casual sex are examples
8. She makes repeated suicidal threats, gestures, or attempts
9. She has a tendency to dissociate or "check out"

Lesbian translation: This grrrl intensely does not like to be alone, and she is rarely single. This is the woman who usually has the next lover lined up before she leaves a current relationship, and if the current partner suspects there is someone in the wings, all the better from her perspective --- she can use your concern about her interest in others as leverage to keep you hooked in. As much as she dislikes being single and alone, she is very uncomfortable with intimacy; if she can play two women at once, she can always cause some drama with the first when things get too close and run to the second for comfort ---- until #2 tries to establish a real connection, at which time she can run back to #1. This woman will break up with you for someone else, and when that doesn't work out, will come back and tell you she was confused and really loved you best all along. You are the best she's ever had---until you are a monster, of course. Wash, rinse, repeat.

Text messaging was made for this woman. She can send you flirty, seductive messages at a rate of a hundred messages a day to help her feel connected and to get assurance from you that she has your attention, all without ever having a real conversation with you. It meets her need for intimacy with distance and distance with intimacy --- but it doesn't translate well into the real world of close contact and real-time, real-world relationships. It does, however, let her keep multiple people on the string at once, and create drama, conflict, and tension among them. Indeed, she may be sending multiple people the same text without letting you know; you may think she is sharing important details of her life with you because you have a special connection. Instead, she is broadcasting to several people, guaranteeing that someone will always be responding.

Having an unstable identity or sense of self can mean a lot of things: she could change her religious orientation, her career goals, her educational plans, or her appearance so dramatically and quickly that it disorients you. This could be part of her appeal---she can be lively and fun in all this changing, but it can also mean she has no stable core inside. This, in turn, means that any life plan you try to make with her may be subject to rearrangement by apparent whim at all times. One significant way this shows up in lesbian communities is in women who are not sure of their sexual identities. They may tell you first that they are lesbian, then that they are bi. They may not be able to give you a clear answer about how it was that they came to date women. They may tell you they have been a lesbian forever but spent years dating and sleeping with men despite their claim to have identified as lesbian at the time. Lesbians often have interesting and complicated stories, but this woman's story will strike you as inconsistent, hard to track, and a little hard to accept at face value.

This woman may invite you home without knowing your last name, just as she did with someone else last night; she may party excessively; she may be a drunk, a drug abuser, or spend-a-holic *and* once she has hooked you, she may expect you to support her habits. If she is a higher functioning borderline woman, she may hold down a responsible job, but be uncertain about her core values. For example, she may ask if you want to sleep with her on a second date, but when you decline she will tell you that she hates "the whole sleep-together-on-the-second-date-become-a-couple-thing." Again, depending on who you are, she may appeal to your sense of fun and adventure, but you will pay the price in drama and heartache.

She may call you and say "I need someone to keep my cats; if "something" happened to me, would you keep them?," implying she might be suicidal when she is feeling left out or rejected because your attention is elsewhere. Her goal is to make you feel sorry for her and turn your attention to her. More directly, she may tell you she will kill herself and try to hold you hostage with this threat; if she is low-functioning, she may attempt suicide and expect you to rescue her and to stay in the relationship as a result. If she is higher functioning, she may say "it's not a matter of 'if' but a matter of 'when;' it is a foregone conclusion that I will kill myself," --thus creating the open-ended prospect that if life doesn't go her way, you may be facing her suicide at any time. Who wants to be responsible for that? Not hyper-responsible you, so you may choose to take extraordinary measures to keep her happy and alive. She may have a lot of tattoos or be a cutter.

In terms of her emotions, this grrrl goes "from 0 to 60 to ballistic," as Annie said, in less than a minute, and back again about as quickly. More than one of my clients has said

"I never know who I will be getting" to describe how quickly the emotional weather can change for this woman. She may be coming on to you one minute and raging at you the next; she may be berating you one minute and five minutes later behave as though nothing happened, all is right with the world, and the two of you should just go on about your day. Whatever is going on for her, she expects you to keep up. She is the woman about whom William Congreve wrote "hell hath no fury like a woman scorned," and she often feels scorned because you looked at her in a way she interpreted as hurtful or didn't respond to a text message within five minutes. Her responses are considered out of proportion to circumstances by most observers; she herself may not understand the intensity of her feelings, so will fabricate facts that could justify this intensity. For example, if she feels jealousy because your work is getting much of your attention, she will make the leap that you are having an affair, accept this as true, and rage at you about it --- even though no affair is happening.

Sometimes, when she is emotionally overwhelmed or overwrought or raging, and sometimes during sex, she "checks out." This can account for why you are amazed that she cannot recall the incident yesterday in which she was calling you horrible names. You are still devastated from it and she is behaving as though it never happened --- possibly because, in her active recollection, it didn't. From there, she accuses you of fabricating or distorting things and over-reacting. This is called projection: when your partner accuses you of doing or saying or feeling the very things that she felt or said or did, without any supporting evidence. For example, borderline girlfriends will often accuse their partners of having affairs or wanting to leave when they themselves are having affairs or planning to leave the relationship.

You can see how the famous lesbian pattern of moving from a first-time meeting, to a sexual encounter, to quickly "becoming an item" and changing one's Facebook relationship status lines up very nicely with the traits that run the show for a person with Borderline Personality Disorder. This is not to say that BPD is always present when two women meet, hook up, and only have eyes for each other; it is to note, however, that in the context of that cultural pattern, it is easy for a woman with BPD to look more normal or functional than she actually is --- and if you don't take some time to get to know her before becoming deeply involved with her, you can find herself in over your head very, very quickly.

Women with Borderline Personality Disorders tend to engage in more come here/go away behaviors than do narcissistic and antisocial women, and the "come here/go away" pattern is a prominent feature of this personality disorder. The title of a famous book about Borderline Personality Disorder is "I Hate You --- Don't Leave Me," (Kreisman 2010) and nicely conveys the bind that women with BPD put their partners in. Women with BPD are dramatic, have difficulty with intimacy, and will drain your energy reserves if you allow it. Although the borderline girlfriend is suffering and uncomfortable herself, and may not consciously intend to cause you harm, she has limited capacity to create a stable, loving, intimate relationship and an immense capacity to pull you off center and away from your own path.

SIFTING AND WINNOWING: DISTINCTIONS AMONG THE DISORDERS

The remaining two personality disorders --- Narcissistic Personality Disorder and Sociopathic Personality Disorder --- also have a good degree of overlap, and share some traits in common with Borderline Personality Disorder, which is why they are all clustered together in the psychologists' handbook. Borderline personality patterns tend to differ from narcissistic and sociopathic personalities in terms of what I think of as their "temperature." Borderline personalities can run very warm; the dramas they create likely involve bids for connection, albeit very toxic ones. Narcissistic and Sociopathic personalities run colder. While you may be manipulated and be deceived by Borderline women, this often happens as a secondary consequence of their desperate attempts to meet their alternating needs for connection and distance. Narcissists and sociopaths are more calculating in their deceptions and manipulations; while people with Borderline Personality Disorder sometimes give evidence of being able to feel empathy, narcissists and sociopaths have much greater limitations in this capacity when you peel back their masks.

Although narcissists and sociopaths often become quite skilled at *portraying* empathy and compassion because this serves them, they have great difficulty taking the role of the other, and see as weak people who don't "play hardball" as they do. They do not feel remorse for their actions, nor for any damage that their actions may cause you.

One really important note about narcissists and sociopaths: strangely, although their capacity for empathy is limited, they often play on your own sympathies to hook you in. This could be sympathy over how badly their exes treated them, sympathy over how badly their parents abused them, or sympathy over some other misfortune. They may not overtly play the victim, which inspires you to see them as evermore noble, for being such extraordinary human beings overcoming such horrible injustices. Early on, their ability to invoke your sympathy this way may make you want to give them everything you believe they deserve. You may hand over your resources to them and feel noble for investing in such a worthy cause. Their more unpleasant, aggressive, and abusive behaviors only emerge when you realize that you are being conned or exploited and begin to try to restructure the balance of power or request some reciprocity.

A second important point: although people who have narcissistic or anti-social personality patterns have a very impaired capacity for empathy, this does not mean they lack other feelings --- such as self-righteousness, for example --- and it doesn't mean they don't express feelings. Unfortunately, however, many of the feelings that sociopaths express are manufactured feelings. Sociopaths often study how emotionally typical people attach to each other, express empathy, express sympathy, etc., so that they can act as though they have these feelings in order to manipulate others. They are often aware that their emotional make-up is very different from that of "normal" people; they become good at covering these differences, which often allows them to give you the impression that they are emotionally literate, spiritually enlightened, compassionate, and able to form attachments. Many sociopaths and narcissists have passed themselves off as gurus, enlightened teachers, and success stories.

THE NARCISSISTIC GIRLFRIEND

You're so vain, I'll bet you think this song is about you. — Carly Simon

Let's take a look at Narcissistic Personality Disorder. Here are the yellow flashing lights that signal your girlfriend is a narcissist:

1. She believes—or wants to believe—that she is superior to others; she exaggerates her accomplishments and expects to be treated as important. She behaves with a sense of entitlement.

2. Her fantasy life centers on her own self-importance

3. She values her time, her ideas, and her resources so disproportionately that she behaves disrespectfully toward the time, money, and resources of others

4. She repeatedly and purposefully takes advantage of other people in order to get what she wants

5. Because she believes herself to be special, she believes she deserves special favors, special possessions, special doctors, and special deals. Whatever she has or decides to do, she is confident that it's the best or the most or the greatest. She lives for the superlatives

6. She requires constant and excessive admiration

7. She is unable or unwilling to notice, relate with, or respond to the feelings and needs of others who do not serve her interests

8. She believes that others are jealous of her special gifts; this is a projection, given that she is herself often envious

9. She is considered by others to be arrogant, haughty, or conceited. Others may refer to her as "Little Miss Know-It-All." When confronted or challenged with factual information that conflicts with what she believes is true, she becomes anxious, defensive, and argumentative; she perceives differences of opinion as personal attacks

10. She expresses the belief that whatever others in her life do, it somehow is directly connected to her

Lesbian Translation: this grrrl may look like a catch, at least from a distance. She may have been very successful professionally; she may have a lot of money, status, or power. She may be drop-dead gorgeous; she certainly believes that she is. While there is something to be said for the old adage that "it's not bragging if it's true," and this woman may be wildly successful in her work, that alone doesn't make anyone great partner material. This woman may have superficial social graces, but likely lacks fundamental kindness, and is too busy telling you about her 180 IQ or how she is "the most popular and high profile executive in her field" to get to know you or take your needs, interests, or desires into account. One of the things she enjoys about you is watching you buy into her stories about her own greatness. If she is interested in you, it is likely because she thinks it will look good for her to be seen with you, or to be connected to you for some reason related to feeding her already inflated ego.

While we all deserve to feel special, especially within the contexts of our relationships and families, the woman with Narcissistic Personality Disorder feels entitled to outright adoration in her relationships and everywhere else she goes. This person differentiates between "regular" people and people like her, whom she believes to be above average in looks, intelligence, creativity, sex appeal or whatever qualities are important to her. If she is suffering or down and out, she may see her situation as especially tragic. When she first turns her attention to you, you may feel flattered; you may feel lucky; you may wonder how you qualified to get into her special elite club.

Narcissists are not always high achievers or living well, however. Sometimes they have stories about their successful previous lives and about their stunning falls from grace --- which are never their responsibility. If a Narcissist was abused as a child, you can bet she considers herself more abused than anyone else, ever, and believes that in order to recover from her trauma, she must be treated only by the most extraordinary of therapists. Your role may be to confirm how extraordinary she is to have survived, and to give her extra special consideration to compensate for the especially difficult circumstances she has found herself in ---

even as she cannot register or appreciate what that requires of you.

If the narcissist is unemployed, she expects someone else to take care of her because she deserves it. If she is housing insecure, she feels entitled to move into the homes of relatives, friends, or lovers and to live rent-free with them for a whole host of reasons ranging from historical economic conditions to the idea that she would do the same for others --- although you rarely see her extending generosity to anyone else. While she is living at others' expense, the narcissist may use a cover story to explain why she isn't working or supporting herself, such as "Their household budget is tight, so I am helping them with the mortgage for awhile." If the narcissist is employed, she expects that because she is who she is, her employer will make exceptions for her, airline companies will upgrade her to first class, and it is perfectly acceptable to leave her hotel rooms in a state of disarray for someone else to clean up.

This grrrl expects you to go along with her program, including her program for you. Any challenge or question you might introduce results in defensiveness, belittling, withdrawal, or retribution. If you get sick, she believes you've done so to inconvenience or undermine her; if you need to focus on working on a project important to you, she will assume your efforts to excel are an effort to compete with her. If you buy a car somehow like hers, she will interpret this as your wanting to be her, even if a million other people are driving that model. If you disagree with her, she will interpret your difference of opinion as an effort to humiliate her.

Part of what makes lovely relationships lovely is each partner' capacity to explore, relate to, respect, understand, and respond kindly to the other's feelings. Narcissists lack this capacity, no matter how skilled they may become at portraying it. If you try to reveal your feelings to them, they can relate if your feelings affirm their sense of superiority somehow. If your feelings don't reflect well on them or their behavior, they may dismiss or belittle you or engage in "victim blame"---telling you that you are responsible for your feelings, have the power to change them, and should---because the narcissist certainly won't change the behavior that is troubling to you. If you are feeling hurt because your girlfriend failed to follow through on planning something special for your birthday, her directive to you to "change your feelings so that you can stop feeling hurt" is clearly a ploy to side-step her responsibility for her hurtful, thoughtless behavior.

Here's an example: A lesbian attributes her trouble getting dates to women feeling intimidated by her success, brilliance, and looks. She assumes that when women don't respond to her overtures that they "always have been crushed out on her" and didn't know what to do with themselves when she expresses interest. She has no insight into how off-putting others find her narcissism; instead, she lives in a narcissistic fantasy that allows her to rationalize why she has such difficulty attracting partners.

Narcissists and sociopaths who are more successful at attracting romantic partners often stage relationships; in the early phases, their presentation centers on flattering you and inducing in you a feeling of being deeply understood, uniquely appreciated, and totally accepted for who you are. They accomplish this by studying you and reflecting you back to yourself, while presenting themselves as people who share your interests, goals, and values, and watering in you the seeds of your desire to build a deeply connected life with a partner who understands you. As the narcissist or sociopath understands you and your needs and vulnerabilities more clearly, she uses her understanding to manipulate you for whatever it is she wants from you. As time goes on, you see more and more of the person behind the façade, while you find it more and more difficult to extricate yourself from a relationship in which you earlier felt adored and appreciated.

The narcissist may try to impress you frequently with her accolades, achievements, or connections, as though she needs to convince you of her specialness, in case you hadn't recognized it before. She also may simply "slip" and convey in everyday life how special she considers herself. She may describe herself as "brilliant" on her own blog. She will behave in ways that we might have called "stuck up" in high school, and eventually she will become boorish. She may well have talent, may be bright, and may have achieved professional or other forms of success, so she is not without credentials. But talents and achievements often speak for themselves, and the kind of real confidence that supports healthy relationships is quiet, unassuming, and gracious. The narcissist's façade of confidence collapses any time she is confronted with information that she doesn't already know, that runs contrary to her beliefs, or that challenges her need to guard her self-concept as someone who is important, expert, and above criticism or reproach in all situations. And when her façade collapses, the narcissist, who feels very small inside, beneath the bluster and bravado, turns ugly.

At some point, after many frustrated attempts to get her attention or to connect with her emotionally, perhaps over the course of years, you will probably realize you need to end your relationship with her for your own sake, no matter how responsible you come to feel you are for her survival or how much you may feel you owe her. Although it is wise to exit without puncturing the narcissist's inflated sense of self, in the end, your absence will make no real difference in her life, because she will quickly find someone else to buy her story and feed her ego --- perhaps at your expense. Given her difficulty in truly attaching to others, a break-up is more a symbolic wound than a heartbreak for a person who is pathologically narcissistic. Besides, breaking up with her allows her to spend more time with the person she loves most: herself.

IS YOUR LOVER A PSYCHOPATH?

"...the pleasure is in gaining and exercising influence over them. I am never infatuated with my possessions, but I am with my exploits. And I can feel possessive of my exploits. I pursue them because they give me a thrill. Will I win them over? What might that look like? Success is valuable only to the extent that it is evidence of my power. As one blog reader said, 'There really is nothing more amusing or exciting or fun than turning a smart, beautiful, resourceful person into a personal plaything.' It is a game, but I am not necessarily interested in the spoils so much as the maneuvering."

---M.E. Thomas (2013, p. 247)

The final stop on our tour through the dramatic personality disorders brings us to the diagnosis of Antisocial Personality Disorder. I will use the common terms "psychopath" and "sociopath" to refer to people who meet a number of the criteria for this diagnosis. Sociopathic traits are more common in the population than you have been led to believe by pop culture or the media; sociopaths are among the people you deal with more regularly than you realize. More common still are people who have sociopathic traits but may not meet the full diagnostic criteria for anti-social personality disorder.

You may have a stereotype of sociopaths as serial killers or mass murders, and many serial killers and mass murders certainly fit the bill. While "having trouble with the law" shows up among the defining characteristics of the

87

disorder, many high-functioning sociopaths do not end up in trouble with the law --- unless they are eventually caught embezzling or laundering money or committing acts of corporate malfeasance. The early and classic descriptions of psychopaths and sociopaths do not include committing murder (solo or serial) as criteria for diagnosing psychopathy (Cleckly 1964; Hare 1999; Anderson 2012).

Some environments reward narcissistic and sociopathic traits, including corporations, the more elite strata of medicine (such as surgery), the music and pro sports industries, and some kinds of operations in the military. You can imagine how having the traits of a sociopath could help a woman climb the corporate ladder. The common belief among people interested in personality disorders is that narcissistic and antisocial personality disorders are on the rise, supported as they are by contemporary social conditions.

If someone's sociopathy were obvious to you at the beginning of the relationship, you no doubt would quietly slip out the side door and make sure you double locked your windows when you got home. The characteristic charm and deceit of the disorder, however, may make it difficult to detect, especially if you have had little previous experience with sociopaths. Think for example about the nurse who thought she had landed a catch when a local lesbian dentist --- her dentist --- began to court her. She was charmed by the dentist's attentiveness and had no awareness that the dentist's previous partner had needed to file a restraining order against her. Three weeks into the relationship, the dentist "let herself in" at the nurse's home, found her credit card bills, and paid them all off. The victim was impressed by this "generous" gesture, while her friends and colleagues sounded like a chorus of Will Robinson's robot: "Warning! Danger! Warning! Danger!" Subsequently, the nurse sold her home, got rid of her pets and possessions, and moved in with the dentist, only to find herself dependent, monitored, controlled, and emotionally and physically abused. Her escape was difficult, her recovery long and arduous.

Let's take a look at the yellow flashing lights associated with the disorder:

1) "Right and wrong" don't really register with her, and are not the standards by which she makes decisions
2) She chronically engages in lying, deceit, and dissembling
3) She uses charm, humor, wit, and seduction to manipulate others---sometimes to achieve a pragmatic goal, like free housing; sometimes simply for the thrill of succeeding at manipulation
4) She may have ongoing legal issues
5) She has a history of violating others' rights
6) She has a history of harming others, possibly including animals
7) She is prone to engaging in intimidation, both subtle and overt, particularly when challenged, rejected, or unable to achieve her goals through charm. She makes threats or efforts to damage partners' welfare, careers, or reputations; in common language: she bullies people
8) She has been known to engage in violent or aggressive behavior, including bodily and property damage.
9) Because of her impaired and limited sense of self, she may not relate to the standard terms of male and female, straight and gay, but instead define her sexuality in terms of conquest and dominance; her lovers and partners come from a fluid set of possibilities across genders, sexual identities, and

races; she may be especially interested in sexual sadomasochism

This woman can justify anything. She can take your money, promise repayment, renege, and convince herself and anyone who will listen that the money she borrowed, stole, or extorted from you was far less than what you should have given her for the privilege of the time you spent together. If she is high-functioning, her charm and wit and power to manipulate, inspire others to give her things. *A sociopath can con you into making your best effort on her behalf and, for a while, feel good about doing it.* Disregard for right and wrong, skillful lying and deceit, strategic charm and wit, and the common talent for manipulating others' sympathies, vulnerabilities, and desires characterize the sociopath's strategies for operating in the world. Bonnie characterizes her former girlfriend this way:

> *She is a con artist. She has a memory that is amazing. She doesn't forget any of the lies that she told. She can keep all of these lies juggling in the air, which makes you think she's not lying because how can anybody remember so many lies and keep them all straight? So, yes, she's con artist.*

If the sociopath is so problematic, why is she so hard to detect?

Some sociopaths are easily identifiable through their overt aggression. It is unlikely that you would have become involved with such a person because you would have been put off by her overt bullying early in a relationship. The sociopath with whom you are likely to get involve masks her penchant to control early on in the relationship as she studies you to determine the ways in which your vulnerabilities may be used against you. The older she is, the more skillful she becomes at this, because she learns from experience how to increase her ability to disarm others' protective defenses. You need to understand that people with sociopathic personalities study non-sociopathic people in order to learn how to imitate and express feelings. Facebook offers sociopaths, like narcissists, a lively new playground, both for studying how emotionally normal people connect and for manipulating others for narcissistic supply and even greater resources. The interior experience of sociopaths differs markedly from the emotional lives of non-sociopathic people. Many sociopaths are aware of this and work hard to compensate for it by studying and then imitating others' emotions in order to manipulate more normal people to feel comfortable connecting with them.

Sociopaths study how others feel, respond, and act, and learn to reproduce the appearance of feeling connection, affection, empathy, and compassion. Then they use these gestures in their relationship with you, expecting that you will trust they are sincere. You believe you are having a relationship; the sociopath in your life believes she is pulling your strings, either just for fun or to achieve some goal she has, like climbing the ladder or living rent-free.

Donna Anderson (2012), a survivor of a marriage to a sociopath, put it this way:

> First, do you have something he or she wants? Second, what are your vulnerabilities? Finally, how can they manipulate you to their advantage?

Sociopaths specialize in targeting vulnerabilities. Most sociopaths are parasites searching for people to live off of, in one way or another. They plow through life, always on the lookout for targets of opportunity. When they find targets — anyone who has anything that they want — sociopaths work quickly to discover the targets' vulnerabilities. Then they pounce.

Kindle Edition, Kindle Locations 1649-1650.

When the lesbian sociopath has trouble with the law or finances, she may ask you to bail her out and have a story about how someone else is responsible for the problem. Because she is charming and knows how to push your buttons, you may well go to collect her from jail, stand by her during her legal problems, or wait for her to finish her time. She chose you because you could be groomed to be loyal and manipulated into her service. Think more broadly here than just stalkers, women who trespass in homes that aren't theirs, women who are violent with children, and people who abuse your credit cards or other financial resources. This may be the woman who drinks and drives without regard for how her behavior puts others at risk. She may be the woman who threatens to ruin your reputation with your colleagues or neighbors because she wants to incite fear and some kind of compliance in you. Like the narcissist, the sociopath is often a bully, whether through physical means or with strategies that are less violent but nonetheless frequently devastating. You may be so smitten with her that you find yourself defending behaviors that you would never engage in yourself. Consider Bonnie's experience:

I didn't want it to end. I didn't want it to be a failed relationship. I had some friends who knew her who gave me some warnings I didn't unfortunately listen to. I wanted to prove them wrong about it. I really did think she was maligned at the time and that they didn't really know her.

She may tell you that she was abused in previous relationships, appealing to your sympathy.

Amanda offered this account:

She told me that she was "called a monster" by her former partner. At the time, I thought it was horrible. I mean, it's a horrible thing to call anyone, let alone to call her, because at that point I still believed that she practiced all of the lovingkindness she expresses to her fans on Facebook. I gave her lots of sympathy and reassurance. Later, both her mask and her gloves came off. I could imagine someone describing her that way if they were at the end of their rope. I almost felt culpable for having assured her that I thought she wasn't a monster, like that gave her permission to test how far she could go with me.

Weirdly, one day she also said to me "You said I am a monster." This was shocking. I am not a name-caller, and have never called anyone a monster, so it was hard to know what to make of this and what to do about it. Was she dissociated and confusing me with someone else? Had it ever happened before? Should I apologize for something I hadn't said and allow that to then stand as the truth, or argue with her? When I pointed out that I hadn't said this, she deflected and said, "well, it feels like that's what you're saying." I hadn't said it, and my feelings were

hurt from being accused, but the expectation was that I would give sympathy and comfort that she felt monsterized. I usually ended up in this one-two process where she would treat me badly and then explain what she had done in some way that was designed to evoke my feeling sorry for some way she was supposedly victimized in the past.

Because she is charming and appears sincere, casual acquaintances hearing the story respond with shock and disbelief, and speculate that the former partner is, in fact a monster herself. Eventually, however, when you move into more intimate contact with the sociopath, you begin to understand how receiving her regular emotional abuse, cognitive distortions, exploitation, and manipulation could bring a partner to use the word "monster" to describe her--- and that this would be considered accurate by anyone who had observed the mask come off.

In *Red Flags of Love Fraud – 10 Signs You Are Dating a Sociopath (2012)*, Donna Anderson notes that while all sociopaths are narcissistic, "the key difference between the two disorders is the degree of inherent malice." The willful intention to frighten, bully, and harm distinguishes sociopaths from narcissists."

People who have anti-social personality disorder are often skilled at justifying their destructive behavior in terms of their victims "deserving it." In one instance, for example, a woman had vandalized her ex-girlfriend's home after the end of the relationship. She threw potted plants onto the sidewalk leading up to the half-million dollar home, destroying the plants, breaking the pottery, and spreading dirt across the walk. She wrote a threat in the dirt that was later photographed and used against her in court, where her ex-girlfriend successfully sought a restraining order. When I asked her about her behavior six months later, she said, "if she didn't want that to happen, she shouldn't have broken up with me. She knows we should be together, and she knows she was asking for it."

SEEING THINGS AS THEY ARE

By now, you should have a sense of how personality disorders are different from mental illnesses, in that they reflect longstanding, inflexible ways of interacting with people and environments, rather than symptoms that come and go, as can be the case with depression, bipolar disorder, schizophrenia, or other forms of mental illness. Although the brain is involved with the patterns associated with personality disorders, the kinds of medicine that benefit people with mental illnesses don't make much difference in the behaviors, perceptions, emotional expression or connection styles of people with personality disorders.

Whereas people who suffer with mental illnesses often seek treatment because their anxiety or depression is making them miserable, people with personality disorders are often very comfortable with how they go about their lives; if there is a problem, the problem is with other people, who don't understand how special, important, or different they are or why their excessive needs for attention and support should be indulged. Sometimes a personality disordered person comes to therapy because a partner has required it. If they find a therapist who reinforces their worldview, based on the accounts they give in therapy, they often stay in treatment because it reinforces their self-image. Most often, the people who come to therapy for personality disorders are not the diagnosable person but their partners or children or parents, who feel as though they are going crazy as a result of how they are suffering from the disordered person's behavior.

Because you have had the misfortune of falling in love with someone who does not have the capacity to be a good partner to you—or to anyone---you may still be in a sympathetic posture toward your beloved. You may have been hoping that if you could understand these patterns better you could somehow intervene to disrupt them and you and your personality disordered girlfriend could live happily ever-after, because when things are good they are very very good -- until they aren't.

It would be wonderful if you could preserve the good times or cleave off the magnificent traits of your disordered girlfriend and keep only the traits that are warm and loving and loyal and interesting and sexy and charming. I understand those wishes, desires, and fantasies on a very intimate level, having walked that walk and hoped those hopes, and having sat with many women who have suffered in exactly the same way. The truth is that unless your significant other understands that her disorder is destroying your relationship, is deeply committed to doing something about it, *and* has access to therapists who have specialized training in working with people who have borderline, narcissistic, or sociopathic personalities, chances are low that your relationship with your personality disordered girlfriend can be transformed. Whatever pattern she is running with you she likely ran with the woman before you, and she will run with the woman following you.

If you want something different for your life, as well you should, deserving of it as you are, you will need to make the changes that make a better, happier, more peaceful life possible for you. The rest of this book is dedicated to helping you do just that --- first, by helping you get a handle on what hooked you into a relationship with a woman who has borderline, narcissistic, or sociopathic behaviors, and second, by helping you develop a strategy for recovering from the damage that you have incurred as a result of having been under-fed, under-loved, unseen, disrespected, hurt, and exploited for so long that you landed here.

Getting Free from Crazy-Making Relationships

IT NEEDS TO BECOME ALL ABOUT *YOU*

That it needs to become all about you is both the good news and the bad news.

Your intimate involvement with someone who has an extremely limited capacity to take other people into account in sustained and meaningful ways drains your life energy, leaving you depleted. Your needle is on E. Your tank is empty. You are worn down and tuckered out, even while you are on edge. You may be so exhausted that you don't realize how exhausted you are. Your body may have begun to reflect the stress of your situation in the form of illness. The people who know you see it, and if you are still in a relationship with a person who is personality disordered, they are worried. If you have recently gone through a break-up with your girlfriend, your friends continue to worry that the relationship will resume. So, it's time for things to become about you: for you to get some rest, for you to re-charge, for you to have your needs and desires and experiences recognized. Before we move on to how to leave and ultimately recover from a relationship with a personality disordered person, let's spend some time excavating what drew you to your disordered girlfriend in the first place: let's make this all about you.

It can be hard to shift focus when your girlfriend has become such a central focus of your attention. Focusing on yourself is the most important thing you can do for yourself right now, nonetheless, whether you are still in a relationship with a disordered woman, on a "break," or sorting through the aftermath of a relationship disaster. In order for you to have your best life moving forward, we need to pause for a little bit to figure out what was going on with you that made you vulnerable to someone so unable to participate authentically in a relationship.

It's easy to explain your involvement in terms of your attraction to your girlfriend's finer qualities --- or what you initially perceived to be finer qualities --- like her vivaciousness, sense of humor, or sex appeal. Still, in your life, this girlfriend functions as a chocolate-covered explosive device. When you are tempted to emphasize your girlfriend's charms over her destructive capacity, remember that "brilliant" "accomplished" "talented" and "vulnerable" can come in stable, non-explosive packages. There really are wonderful, lovely, brilliant women in the world who are stable and kind. Look around your friendship and work circles, and you will likely see many of them. Look in the mirror, and you will see one more. So, despite the lesbian population pressure that leads women to believe that they have no better option than to stay with an abusive or exploitive girlfriend, trust that it is possible to meet women who are interesting to you without bringing chaos and destruction into your life.

This leads us to the question: What has been going on with you that you would sign up for, settle for, and continue to hang onto a woman whose good qualities are appealing, but whose cruelty and drama and manipulation, whose capacity to make your life a nightmare, whose pattern of either failing to notice your suffering or failing to care about it should outweigh any positive quality that anyone could imagine? Why would you allow this chaos or deep dissatisfaction to continue in your life when there exist peaceful, happy alternatives?

COULD IT BE THE SEX?

In this chapter, I am going to provide you with some possible explanations for your vulnerability to and participation in a toxic, crazy relationship that didn't uplift your spirit or bless your life or benefit your people or community. We'll go beyond the ways that homophobia and heterosexism and lesbian population pressure might make us vulnerable, in general, to toxic relationships, and we'll explore some additional ideas from social and clinical psychology so that you can cultivate an even richer understanding of your own vulnerabilities. While the solution to your situation may appear quite simple to an outsider ("Just back away, friend"), it probably doesn't feel that way to you at the moment. And "simple" does not always translate into "easy," even if you have already put "make an exit plan" on your to-do list.

You found this book because you have spent countless hours and maybe significant cash trying to figure out what was going on with your girlfriend. Does she have PTSD? Does she have ADHD? Does she have a medical illness that could explain her behavior? It's clear you are a contemplative person searching for answers. Now that you have some understanding of what personality disorders are and how they operate, I would like to help you explore the factors that allow you to be attracted to a woman who can cause so much pain in your life. You need to understand why, instead of ruling her out as prospective partner, you have invited her in and continue to try to make things work against incredible odds.

IGNORING THE EMERGENCY EARLY WARNING SYSTEM

Nearly every woman in a toxic relationship with a personality-disordered partner can identify warning signs of trouble from the early days of the relationship. Very few women say, "I had no clue that she was trouble." Some felt unease but failed to recognize early on how deeply disturbed a partner was. Many looked past warning signs because they wanted to offer the girlfriend generosity of spirit; they assumed the best despite observations that contradicted their assumptions, usually with the hope that the nagging voice suggesting trouble could be mistaken. Here are some stories of those early signals:

There were a whole bunch of [warning signs] even before anything started. Even one of the first times we went out in a group, the way she was looking at me made me uncomfortable. It was kind of this boring [into me] look. And then I talked to some [other] people and I'd start getting the jealous attitude thing already. Then I started doing the dance of trying to explain myself: 'I am just talking...' It was happening right away.

I had only seen her four times. She calls me up one night and she wants to know if I was working that night or the next day. I said no. She was wondering if I wanted to come over to her house. It was late. I was already in bed. She wanted me to have sex with her. She told me it would be the best night I ever had. I said, 'You don't even know me. How do you know it would be the best thing? How would you even know what I wanted?' And I laughed and I said, 'No. If I was maybe 20, I would maybe jump in the car and come over there, but no.' And then she was mortified.

The warning signs were all over the place. When we first started spending time together, she told me that she had spent time in jail for beating up previous girlfriends, and she's not that person anymore.

It had to have been in that first week. She played softball on Thursday nights. So I went to watch her play. And she had told me that she played softball with her ex, but they had separated a year before from a live-in three-year relationship. So, I'm like "that's not a big deal." You know how our people are. We always have to fight like hell to be "friends" with our exes, good or bad. So I went to watch the game, and I didn't make a big show of it. I just showed up and sat in the bleachers. So when the team came in from the outfield –and I knew who her ex was because she had shown me a picture--the ex just shot right past the dugout and went straight to her car. And I'm like, "I wonder why?" Of course, after the game she came and told me that AJ got upset [that I was there]. Later, I texted her, "When you clean up whatever is going on for that reaction to happen, let me know, because I am just not interested [in drama]." She showed up later that night, and she brought me a little gift. And she said "I don't want our potential relationship to be fucked up because of my ex. I'd like the opportunity to fuck it up myself." I had no idea how true those words would come to be. I thought, "OK, fair enough." And she said that AJ was possessive and and and and…so I felt I had been reassured by her that it was a weird dynamic on AJ's part.

I had signals right away which I chose to ignore. At one of the softball games when she stopped to talk to me, she actually left her beer cooler sitting next to me so every time she needed a beer she had to come back to the cooler, which was sitting next to me. In that conversation she mentioned that she was not a drinker, she told me she didn't drink as much s her friends. She would have a few beers at softball but she wasn't a regular drinker. As I got to know her, I discovered that almost everything revolved around drinking. The warning signal occurred later, when drinking was a component of almost everything we did. She also told me she had quit smoking but after a few weeks of dating, the cigarettes were quite evident. She told me that she was stressed because of the relationship with her ex, and her ex coming back, so she was turning to these things because of the stress, but it was unusual for her. And I wanted to believe that, so I did.

Some of her closest friends I got to know and they told me to run. They would say, 'I am a very good friend of hers, I have known her my entire life, and I suggest that if you want to save your sanity you should get out of the relationship.' And most of these people had been involved with her in the past.

With the benefit of time, distance, and experience, the survivors of these relationships regret having ignored such signs that trouble was on the horizon. Most have become more adept at understanding the significance of the early warning signals and choosing not to proceed in relationships where they are present. In retrospect, it becomes easier to see both the dynamics and the personal vulnerabilities that contribute to our tendency to look the other way.

REWARDS & PUNISHMENTS

Sociopaths pour on the charm, proclaim their love and get you into bed. Then, as you become more and more attached, they disappear. Or they ignore you. Or they pick a fight. What are they doing? They are intensifying your love bond. Just as sociopaths instinctively know to hook you with pleasure in the beginning of the relationship, they also know that they can make you even more attached by threatening the relationship. This seems counterintuitive. If someone is giving you a hard time, why would you want to continue your involvement? The answer comes from addiction research. Scientists have discovered that although pleasure is required to establish a behavior pattern, it is not required to maintain it. So once a love bond is formed, it stays in place, even when the loving behavior disappears.

-- Donna Anderson (2012-06-05). Red Flags of Love Fraud - 10 signs you're dating a sociopath (Kindle Edition, Kindle Locations 2344-2354).

There's a classic model of human behavior in psychology that argues that we do what we do because we get rewarded for doing it. It also argues that when we are consistently punished or get a negative response for a behavior we stop doing it. To use a simple example: if we go to the Michigan Women's Music Festival and have a great time --- say we meet someone wonderful and enjoy her company all week, the weather is perfect, the performers are all in fine form, we get a great tan, see old friends, and find an herbal cure for our cats' allergies -- all of the expense and hassle of getting there are positively reinforced, and we are likely to return. If we go to the Michigan Women's Music Festival and have a horrible time --- say, our date runs off with someone else, we end up with an intestinal parasite someone brought from Central America, the women on the sanitation crew go on strike in solidarity with Camp Trans so that there are no Porta-Janes available when the parasite hits, and it's 104 degrees out for a week ---we are negatively reinforced. And we become far less likely to feel good about spending money, time, and energy on this event in the future. Scenario one: positive reinforcement; scenario two, negative reinforcement.

Consistent positive reinforcement helps to strengthen behaviors --- the dog sits for a treat; your girlfriend does the chore you hate for the treat of your appreciation. Consistent negative reinforcement works to extinguish behaviors --- ignoring the dog's whining while you eat will teach her begging doesn't pay, and ignoring the woman who is over-texting you will eventually extinguish her efforts to make contact. Consistency is key in the effort to shape the behavior of sentient beings, according to this theory, which originates in the work of classical psychologists (Watson & Raynor, 1920; Pavlov, 1927). Think about how many times a woman has shaped your behavior by giving you positive or negative reinforcement, and you'll see that there is some merit to the argument.

So far so good. But what happens when a person (or dog or cat or chicken) gets mixed signals? This is called "intermittent reinforcement." Let's go back to Michigan. In Scenario 1, you had a revolutionary good time, so of course

106

you did everything you could to go back. For three years you returned, and for three years, you had a great time. In year four, you got Shigella, your partner ran off with someone, the weather was miserable, and the debates about monogamy got on your nerves, especially because they supported your partner's infidelity. It was a bad, bad year. Still, with three good years to the festival's credit, it has a good track record with you, so you might be willing to go back. You think it's worth the risk. You return, despite this anomalous suffering and drama, and have a nice time. You continue to go back through the ecstatic years and the nightmare years, and sometimes you wonder why. You have been intermittently reinforced.

Your new rescue dog begs for your food when you are eating at the table. You don't enjoy this, so you ignore her begging, thinking that consistently not giving her the food she is asking for will extinguish this behavior. After three days of not giving her any scraps, you are beginning to feel worn down. Besides, she is so cute. And what you're having is a nice steak, which is really fine for dogs to eat. So, you make an exception. To yourself you say, "Okay, I have steak only twice a month. When I have steak I will give Fifi a scrap." Fifi loves her steak, of course. And now that you have given her hope, Fifi will return to your table night after night, hoping against hope that tonight is the night that you will recreate for her the nirvana world that includes steak.

If your experience with your partner were all bad, you wouldn't stay. If it were all good, you wouldn't be so miserable right now. If Fifi's experience with you were that you never, ever gave her table scraps, you would have a well-behaved dog, instead of a pathetic needy beggar. With human beings, the kisses, the positive words, and the occasional table scraps of affection keep people coming back for more; they keep our mammal brains hopeful that what we experienced once we could experience again, if we keep showing up or, like Fifi, just keep hanging in there, even when we are being ignored, starved, or tormented. You are a smart woman: you see where I am going with this.

Many lesbians struggling with these toxic relationships say that when the relationship is good it is *very good* and that it is difficult to walk away from because those moments are so meaningful – and they provide some hope that things are better or are getting better and will be better from now on. The table scraps tend to be good steak, after all, and they feed you with the powerful elixirs of hope and relief.

It was very good sometimes. She was very passionate, which was kind of a new experience too. And I loved the dancing. The sex was kind of spectacular. Which would make it really freaking sad. You think about that and it's like "holy cow. It's that intense. Cool, you know? And that would compensate some for it.

In the beginning I think I kept thinking that first we would talk it through. And we'd talk it through and then she would have these epiphanies and then she would be back to this caring thing. But she would be so quick on this getting mad or this "I'm breaking up with you" thing, a lot of times I got to the point where I just knew that she was coming back. That it just wasn't the way it was, or these were just words. But they were still hurtful.

She was always there when I needed her. She helped me on the farm. We slept well. It was so nice to be held. She was dependable. She also helped me get a job where she was working. Then we became sexual. I needed someone

reliable. They show up and they're so helpful and they are there when you need them. And you rely on them. And then they go really wacko. And it's really hard.

Behaviorism looks at observable behaviors. So, from within its model we can only try to understand what we see, as though we were watching a videotape of your behavior or your interaction with your girlfriend. Analyzing the video, without the audio playing, we might be able to see you looking pleased and happy when your girlfriend hugs you at 6 pm and confused or frightened or shut down when she is throwing things at you at 6:30. Watching the video, we might wonder why you don't just walk away when the throwing of objects starts. First, we see that your experience is not consistent. If your girlfriend were always throwing things and screaming, always cruel, always obnoxious or bombastic, it would be very easy for you to go. But she's not, which is why it is not so easy to walk away. Any minute, the winds could shift again.

The intermittent reinforcement also creates something we can't see simply by looking at the video. I believe that intermittent reinforcement adds an element of intrigue or mystery to one's interaction with a personality disordered person; it creates a puzzle; it is difficult to understand. If you are a curious person, or a "fixer" ---and many people with personality disorders are attracted to competent types --- intermittent reinforcement likely activates both your curiosity and your desire to figure things out so that you can fix them, with the goal that instead of dealing with a GF who is only sometimes reliable and sometimes honest and sometimes available and sometimes interested in

Getting Free from Crazy-Making Relationships

you, you will be with a girlfriend who is all of those things all of the time.

Can you see now how *your continuing to respond to your GF's inconsistent behavior creates intermittent reinforcement of that very behavior in her?* Sometimes when she's a jerk, you confront her; sometimes when she's a jerk, you try to just ignore the behavior. Sometimes when she's a jerk you just cave in and give her what she wants. She breaks up with you and tells you, "I am done;" you accept this. When she starts showing up again a week later, however, you allow her to re-enter your life. As a result, her inconsistent behavior with you gets reinforced by you. We can complain about the inconsistent behavior of the personality disordered partner, but where we need to focus is on our own inconsistent responses to that behavior. Fifi keeps coming back to the table, acting like a maniac and expecting steak because she knows you love her (and have steak); every so often, when she gets a morsel, whether because you can't take the drama anymore or because you want to reward a glimmer of good behavior, you are relieved that she is relieved for a moment, and you have just contributed to the dynamic that is causing you to suffer.

When I ask lesbians who have been in relationships with personality disordered partners how often the relationship ended, they often laugh in exasperation. Here are some examples of answers to this question:

> **Thousands! Thousands. It was serious. It was a lot. It would happen all the time. Every time we'd have a fight she would break up with me. I would say, fine. And then she would call. It was like it didn't happen. It was like it was just words to her. To me it actually means something, but to her it's just these words." So then I would say,**

"okay, for six months you can't break up with me."

Are you kidding? It happened so many times it was ridiculous. She was the first to break up with me. She made her decision to stay with her ex-partner (that she had gotten back with while we were dating). She did that when I was on a trip to FL. When I came back she let me know she was going to stay with the ex. I thought it was over. She called within a couple of weeks and said "No, the ex and I are done. She is moving out." And we went through that over and over and over.

In these examples, you can see the beleaguered partners taking back the girlfriends who have cheated on them or called them names or exploited them or stressed them out. We do this for all kinds of unfortunate reasons. What the partners hope for is a return to romance, an increase in stability, and a reduction in drama. By reuniting with a partner who has behaved in a toxic way, however, we achieve just the opposite, because we are rewarding the behavior. From a behaviorist perspective, it is no wonder that the break-up/make up cycle so common in abusive relationships across all sexuality categories repeats itself again and again. Lesbians may be inclined to think of "domestic violence" or "intimate partner violence" as happening only in cross-sex relationships, in which men are physically violent with women. This bias may prevent us from accurately recognizing that the three-stage Cycle of Abuse---build up/beat-up/make-up ---- frequently replicates itself in the emotional dynamics of abusive same-sex relationships, whether or not they involve physical violence (Walker 1979; Renzetti 1992). In one relationship described here, the abusive partner who had previously been in jail on battery charges didn't hit her latest girlfriend, but told her that she

wanted to provoke her into making the first contact so that
she could feel justified in responding violently. You can
imagine the challenges facing police officers who respond to
calls involving same-sex couples in which this dynamic is
present.

When the abusive behavior rises to the level of illegal
or criminal behavior, or involves financial exploitation or
other legal issues, such as property ownership disputes and
child custody concerns, women in same-sex relationships
often face difficult decisions about whether to turn to the law
enforcement or judicial systems for support in the pursuit of
their rights. Aware of the history of discrimination against
women in general and lesbians in particular in these systems,
women weigh the costs and benefits of taking legal action,
including calling the police. Victims try to calculate the
likelihood that seeking redress will improve their situations
rather than make the situation worse. One woman I
interviewed had experienced multiple dramatic events
involving a former date and chose in each instance to tough
things out on her own instead of involving police:

*Soon after we start sleeping together, I wake up in the middle of
the night. She is holding me down. Dogs are freaking out.
There is broken glass. And she is screaming in my face [about
having an affair with my boss] and holding me down. Throwing
things. Yelling and screaming. Packing up her shit. She grabs
her dog. She leaves. Then she comes back and it starts all over
again. I tried to convince her that I am not having an affair
with anybody, and my boss is married to another woman, so
why? What she wants is for me to hit her so she can pound me.
And I know this. I just instinctively know that that's what she
wants. She outweighs me by at least a hundred pounds, and she*

says she's afraid of me because I'm stronger because I run a farm. I was petrified of her. So she left. Finally. Again.

We were on the farm, out in the middle of nowhere, and I am not going to call the cops because Lesbian Relationship Gone Wrong wouldn't go over well with them.

This survivor intended to never see her date again, but the date began harassing her. The survivor attempted to placate her ex-girlfriend by spending limited amounts of time with her, thinking that "trying to be friends" at a superficial level would limit her escalations. Unfortunately, this strategy provided positive reinforcement to the personality-disordered woman, who became increasingly controlling:

She showed up. It must have been a weekend morning because I'm in my bathrobe. I instinctively grabbed the phone and put it in the pocket. It's a good thing I did. She takes my cell phone and wings it across the room and shatters it. She takes the other home phone and does the same thing. Takes a big glass jar full of change and throws it against the fireplace---glass, money everywhere.

Incidents like this continued for more than a year.

Somewhere in all of that she showed up at my door with chocolate and flowers. And I just laughed. I said "that's so typical." It's the perfect abuse cycle. I used to teach this!

Police were never called. Why? Being ashamed. And being a dyke. The judgment in that. I was worried about what the police would think. "Bunch of crazy dykes," blah, blah, blah. Had it been a man, I would have certainly called the cops.

So, intermittent reinforcement serves to keep lesbians holding onto the idea that their disordered partners can somehow be inspired to "just be nice" consistently if we can only figure out the formula. It keeps lesbians hooked into relationships that have good moments in the context of daily misery. Ironically, when we don't draw the line and hold it in the face of toxic behavior, for whatever reason we might have, *we also reinforce the very behavior we would like to extinguish in disordered partners.* The woman above unwittingly reinforced her date's behaviors for more than a year. When she did threaten to call the police, her date said "Go ahead; I'll be out of here before the squad car leaves the station." Eventually, after the date had broken into her home, stalked her, and threatened her repeatedly without repercussion, she caused my interviewee to lose her job in their common workplace. At that point, she petitioned the court for a restraining order. "I had nothing left to lose at that point," she says. Unfortunately, the restraining order wasn't granted --- because the police hadn't been called to the scene of any of the earlier events. Nonetheless, the date's harassing, intimidating behaviors finally stopped. Why? My interviewee puts it plain: "She realized I finally meant business."

THE ROOTS OF VULNERABILITY

The idea that intermittent reinforcement is part of how we get hooked with personality disordered partners makes a lot of sense --- behaviors that are intermittently reinforced are the hardest to break. Still, some women would notice inconsistent behavior --- or cruelty, or narcissistic self-centeredness, or manipulation, or a disconnect between what a woman says and what she actually does --- early in a relationship and simply walk away. The women interviewed here didn't, as is the case for many of you reading this book right now. What are some other possible ways you might have been or might be vulnerable?

One theory about why some lesbians become "U Haul Magnets," as one of my recent Lesbian Dating Seminar workshop participants labeled herself, is that when some of us cross paths with personality disordered partners, we are vulnerable to them because they bring up some unhealed family dynamic for us. Perhaps you have a parent who was personality disordered and with whom you have "unfinished business." Perhaps your prospective love match felt deeply familiar to you or like "coming home." That sensation can be a very compelling one, until we re-connect with the truth that home may have been chaotic, dysfunctional, or invalidating. It may be that the personality disordered person has gotten a sense of where our buttons are hidden, and uses that knowledge to make herself more appealing to us as a prospective mate.

Many partners report that in their relationships with disordered women they find their own behavior regressing: folks who don't yell find themselves raising their voices; folks who are not violent find themselves wanting to throttle their girlfriends. One woman who had dated a personality disordered woman for a year said to me, "I used to watch crime shows on TV and couldn't understand how someone could stab somebody else 16 times and feel okay about it; now I get it."

Sometimes it seems to me that a woman having these feelings is similar to a person watching a train wreck over and over again: glued to the scene, fascinated by it, disturbed by it, at risk of harm from it, and completely able to simply turn and walk away: in essence, frozen. Not every person who has a personality disordered parent becomes personality disordered herself, and not every non-disordered child of a

115

personality disordered parent finds herself fascinated by personality disordered people. But there are many among those who get caught in these relationships who can identify a difficult relationship with at least one caregiver. When they are in a romantic relationship with a personality disordered woman, they stay longer than makes sense. Like a dependent child with no capacity to escape, they feel that they cannot leave --- and are responsible for how the other person is treating them.

Children assume that parents should love and care for them, so when that doesn't happen, children often conclude there is something unlovable or unworthy about themselves, and often they make desperate efforts to secure their care-givers' attention and affection. That primordial, original drama is activated in relationships between personality disordered women and their partners:

I'm the oldest of 7 kids. I am a caretaker. I know that I am. And I like it. It does make me feel good to help somebody, to be able to take care of somebody. The one thing I really appreciated about my relationship with Sally was that we took care of each other equally. And that's what I keep thinking that I'm looking for, and that's what I keep thinking that's what I am going to be getting. And I keep thinking that you can prove that to her. But it doesn't change.

I think a lot of it had to do with doing stuff to go yes, I am worth it. I've never said the word so many times in my life. I just wanted her to be nice. If I do this now, now will you be nice? I wasn't asking for a lot. All I wanted was, I just wanted enough. I'm not looking for millions, I just want enough. I wanted her to care enough to not talk to me that way. All I want is a hug before you leave. That's all: I just wanted enough.

I would make her funky ass espresso before she left for work, and she would go into a tirade of how I didn't do it right. Okay, so then it became a critique of this, this, this. So I would do what I could. I know it makes me sound like such a dumbass. When it was good it was good. If she was always mad at me, it must be my fault.

Partners of personality disordered people often feel a kind of desperation to preserve the relationship that reminiscent of the life-or-death dynamic of infants' dependency on their parents. Although much of this can be attributed to intermittent reinforcement, and lesbian population pressure, it is worthwhile to consider whether these relationships enact dysfunctional dynamics with disordered parents. Over and over, I am struck by how much time and effort partners of people with personality disorders invest in holding onto these relationships and trying to fix them, when the partners are so clearly abusive and so clearly not investing reciprocally. Eventually, that burden becomes exhausting, both physically and emotionally. One interviewee put it like this:

They always talk about that with great risk, comes great reward, and working for things, and the early bird getting the worm. Then you go: 'I've gotta work hard if I want something *really* good.' And then on the other side of it is this: you shouldn't have to work that fucking hard to be loved.

BEING IN THE WRONG PLACE AT THE WRONG TIME

Life circumstances constitute a third element that makes lesbians vulnerable to women with personality disordered traits. At some times in our lives we simply are more resilient, and at other times we are more vulnerable. Some women who historically have made good relationship choices may become vulnerable to personality disordered women at times of extreme stress. Several women I interviewed, for example, got involved with their disordered partners in the wake of periods of significant life stress or disruptive losses or heartbreak. Such events might include the death of a beloved partner; the death of parents; times of significant upheaval or transition: job loss or relocation, or finishing degrees, starting careers, or dealing with a life threatening illness. Sometimes, there's simply a pragmatic push to settle down:

> *There was the fact that I had waited over five years to bring anyone into my kids' lives, and now I had done that. Not only would I fail as a companion/partner, but also as a parent who had brought someone into their lives if this didn't work out.*

> **I was maybe feeling a little desperate. I had left a marriage. Several dating relationships had not panned out. I had done a fair amount of dating and internet dating that had not panned out, and it was time for me to find that person.**

> *[When my partner died two months after her diagnosis with ovarian cancer] I was really lost. When she died, we were standing on the top of the ladder of everything we were shooting for, and that was just pulled out from under us. [Two years later, when I got involved with Janelle], the warning signs were there. But I was in this weird not-myself place.*

118

Sometimes lesbians start relationships with personality disordered women when a primary relationship is faltering or has become hyper-stable and less interesting or intimate than during the honeymoon years; Borderline women in particular are attracted to being involved with "married" people, and a married woman who doesn't know how to salvage her long-term relationship or exit it gracefully may find herself deeply attracted both to the borderline woman's overtures and to the frisson of secrecy that results from an affair. Predictably, when the partnered woman ends her relationship to be with her exciting new disordered partner, the disordered woman's fear of intimacy arises in response to the formerly partnered woman's new availability and she bolts, with a wake of destruction and heartache in her path.

INTEGRATING ELEMENTS OF VULNERABILITY TO TOXIC PARTNERS

Put these elements together, and what might a person especially vulnerable to personality disordered partners look like? She might look like a person who had one or two parents who were unavailable, disconnected, or invalidating, and who left her with unfinished business, unanswered questions, or unmet needs. Those old forms of hunger make her susceptible to being willing to work harder than someone else to get the feeling of connection that her disordered or unavailable parent deprived her of. She may do just fine in relationships with non-disordered people, but find herself especially compelled by a disordered partner whose traits line up in some significant relational way with those of her disordered or unavailable parent. On top of this vulnerability, throw in a few challenging life circumstances that disorient her away from good judgment and make her open to the attentions of someone who initially seems very interested in her, and she is vulnerable.

Add to this the reinforcing power of the table scraps of intermittent intense affection, followed by distancing behaviors, or the appearance of offering unconditional acceptance and love followed by disrespect, contempt, intrusiveness, or maliciousness --- and we can see a pretty decent recipe for receptivity to a person with a disordered personality. Amplify this further still by lesbian population pressure --- the awareness that partner choices are limited --- and a woman may be disinclined to listen to that still small voice that even in the beginning many women hear whispering like Will Robinson's Robot: "Warning! Warning! Danger, Danger!"

IF SHE CAN FIND YOUR HOOKS, YOU MIGHT TAKE THE BAIT

So far, we have thought about some of the broad factors that might have made you vulnerable to getting involved with someone with a personality disorder that has made your life miserable. Before you start feeling bad about yourself, remember a couple of things: 1) you were not the first and you will not be the last fine woman of whom this girlfriend will take advantage or torture; 2) the fact that you may have some special vulnerabilities does not mean that you are responsible for your girlfriend's disordered behavior. You are responsible for your own behavior, as she is responsible for hers. The fact that she has exploited your vulnerabilities speaks for itself. What it suggests about you is that you need to develop better skills at identifying and screening out women who will run dysfunctional patterns with you.

So within the context of these broad variables --- population pressure, unresolved family issues, life circumstances and intermittent reinforcement, what are some even more specific ways lesbians get hooked in these dysfunctional relationships? We'll spend the rest of this chapter looking at some of the common hooks that keep women on the line.

What are hooks? I think about them as the sticking points that make it harder for women to walk away from relationships in which they are clearly being mistreated. Many "hooks" come from family rules, assumptions, and expectations about what a good partner or a good person does. For example, in my family, an implicit agreement is "we don't abandon sick people." So, for me to walk away from someone when she is ill, even when her disorder causes her to mistreat me, runs deeply counter to my socialization, my childhood programming. You can see how someone whose behavior becomes associated with illness, or someone who is chronically ill, can appeal to my care giving desires, and create situations in which I find it difficult to extricate myself, even if I am being mistreated or exploited. I can always chalk the toxic behavior up to illness, and what people in my family do with ill people is take care of them.

Everyone has hooks. Everyone's hooks relate to what we saw and experienced at formative moments in our lives; we either aspire to operate in ways like those we admire or in ways that distinguish us from people we don't respect. We may have seen our parents stay with each other "come hell or high water" and, as a result, we have come to value "staying power." Like not abandoning ill people, being able to persist in relationships can, indeed, be a laudable quality. However, if we allow ourselves to be rushed into coupledom and then realize that our girlfriend is regularly unkind or overly demanding or constantly exploiting our resources, our very fine qualities and values can be turned against us.

I could envision being with her. For a long time. She wanted to be with me…for the rest of her life. So we would talk about the rest of our lives, getting old together, the whole bit. But there was this huge....I think it's from how my parents were. There weren't exactly happy together, but they stayed together. That was just how it was. It's that Catholic thing. You just...even if you aren't tremendously happy, you just stay. And I think it was something along those lines; I just kept thinking that you just work at it...we're just having some problems....So I wanted it to be that way. But it wasn't.

We stop listening to our inner wisdom and continue to trudge through the relationship. We may be operating in alignment with our values, but these values were designed to do good, not harm; in toxic environments, they may have the opposite effect, like medicine that is used in ways it was intended to be used. In essence, we are hooked.

So, what are some of your hooks, the feelings that have kept you engaged in a relationship that is more like a nightmare than a dream come true?

Here are some of the issues that lesbians have reported as keeping them hooked in crazy-making relationships. Check to see if any of them sound familiar:

"Her life was a disaster; if I didn't take care of her, I didn't know who would, and I didn't want whatever happened to her on my conscience."

"She needed me; I thought if I left, I would feel dishonorable."

"If I ended it, I thought she would kill herself."

"I recognized that she was not well, but people who are not well need our kindness, not our judgment or rejection."

"I loved her."

"Being with her was exciting and different and made me feel alive---until I was so exhausted I wanted to be dead."

"I realized this was a nightmare, but her kid had become attached to me, and I now feel responsible for him."

"She is fabulous---smart, gorgeous, rich—I thought I really didn't deserve to be with someone who has all of those great qualities. I figured you have to take the bad with the good."

"She invited me to move in within a couple of weeks, and I did. I gave up my apartment and quit my job so I could go to school full-time -- it seemed very supportive at the time. I realize now that it was a mistake. I became dependent---and I was star-struck for awhile. I thought I could deal with her narcissism. She often joked that putting up with her is a small price to pay for the luxuries she shared with me, but there's some truth to it. What did she get out of it? Having a girlfriend is simply an ego boast---it just happened to be me; it could have been anybody who met her criteria and could deal with her."

"I am flattered that someone as young and beautiful and smart and creative as she is was interested in me."

"She can't survive without me."

"It must have been a past-life thing."

"She made me feel needed."

"I need someone to do the things in life that I am not confident I can do; even though she makes me miserable, and the relationship is twisted, I stayed in it because I was afraid to be alone."

"We are so legally entangled now that if I leave, I will lose everything. And she knows it. I am completely trapped."

"Other people left her in cruel ways---or so she said; I didn't want to be one more person who contributed to her distrust of human kind."

"I am not such a great catch myself; beggars can't really be choosers."

"I learned from my parents that relationships are difficult but that the honorable thing to do is to stay, no matter what."

"She slept around, but I think she can't really help herself; she told me that I'm the one she loves, so I hung in here while she works out her issues."

"Because I had the ability to give, it seemed wrong of me to withhold what she needed. She is a person in my life, after all."

"She is vulnerable; she had a hard childhood and has been in difficult relationships. I understand this; I get her. When she was mean, I saw it as just a reflection of how scared and vulnerable she is---and I thought my love could make a difference."

BREAKING THROUGH THE FOG

Even though each person's story is a bit different, you can see the common themes that show up repeatedly in these hooks. We could probably boil them down to three or four. Many people who have been in relationships with personality disordered people, and many therapists who have worked with them, use the acronym "FOG" to represent three common reasons people in relationships with personality disordered significant others don't simply end these relationships. "FOG" stands for "fear, obligation, and guilt." People fear what will happen to their partner or what their partner will do to them if they end things---as bad as things are, they predict that things could get worse; they feel obligated to buck this person up, to underwrite her needs, to make her life easier or better; and they feel guilty or worry about feeling guilty if they terminate the relationship.

Beyond fear, obligation, and guilt keeping us hooked in, of course, is the power of connection—of being needed, of feeling as though we belong to someone and they to us, of being part of a couple or family or pack. This shows up throughout the hooks; as little as our needs for connection may be met in these toxic relationships, the unresolved childhood attachment problems and the intermittent reinforcement keep us on the hook of hope ---- repeatedly leaping for the bait that somehow things will turn out okay and we can finally move toward the Happily Ever After part of the program.

SHE MAY BE THE CAUSE, BUT YOU HAVE THE SOLUTION

Being in a relationship with someone with a serious personality disorder, you may be suffering lots of agitation, disorganization, and lack of focus; you may be experiencing depression, anxiety, and exhaustion. You may be jeopardizing your job by being unable to stay centered or by cutting time away in order to deal with your girlfriend's constant crises, craziness, or drama. You may be over-working or drinking more than you should to numb yourself out to the reality of being around her. You may be emotionally down for days because she has rejected you again, without explanation, and then agitated for several days more because she has come circling back as though nothing ever happened. Your friends may have stopped coming around or may have told you that they can't hear any more of your stories about your disordered girlfriend. Although your girlfriend's pathology may well be related to many factors over which she had little control, her current behavior perpetuates abuse and exploitation. As an adult, her behavior is her responsibility, as your behavior is yours. Your responsibility is to cultivate your own sanity, safety, well-being, and health.

Because your life was better before her arrival, it is easy to believe that your girlfriend is the problem, and to keep your mind occupied with her issues, her problems, her behaviors and how to fix them. One of my interviewees, a self-declared care-giver, told me, "I feel like she needs somebody like me to save her silly ass, you know, 'cause she is kind of a disaster on her own." Others reported that they feared disordered girlfriends would commit suicide or end up living on the streets, uninsured, and unemployed if they ended the toxic relationship. Some feared an escalation in threats, manipulations, extortion, and retaliation. Although all of these behaviors are problematic, they are also all beyond

126

your control. *It isn't so much your girlfriend's disorder but your response to it that is turning your own life into "kind of a disaster."*

The difference between the two of you is that despite your vulnerabilities, you have the ability to do things differently. Part of what defines personalities as disordered is the chronically inflexible ways a person responds to the environment; less disordered people are able to grow and change and adopt new strategies for getting their needs met when the strategies they are using aren't effective. In addition, less disordered people take responsibility for their behaviors, and are motivated to change, whereas more disordered people feel no need to change because they are not the problem, from their perspective, and they are not responsible for the things that happen to them. So, the good news is that as much as this relationship may have depleted and disoriented you, you do have immense capacity for change and growth. You can recognize that using the approach you've been using up until now and expecting to get a different outcome constitutes its own kind of insanity. And you can come to the conclusion that you need to do something differently if you want your life to change.

For all of the ways you may be healthier and more functional than your disordered girlfriend, the other truth is this: whether your girlfriend is borderline or narcissistic or sociopathic, she will move on from your relationship largely unscathed. Because these personality disorders all fundamentally reflect difficulties in connecting with and caring for other human beings, this girlfriend is likely only connected with you in superficial ways, no matter the intensity that she initially showed up with or the ways she has learned to mimic what less disordered people do to give the impression of intimacy. She may raise a ruckus because you have wounded her ego or activated her abandonment issues. She may cause you trouble. But the chances that you will damage her by ending a relationship with her are low.

One sociopath who created havoc in the lives of several women told me, "I enjoy people when they are around, but I don't miss them when they die or are gone." So, put to rest your desire to do no additional damage to someone you believe has already been damaged, if that has you hooked into this relationship. While this is an important and ethical concern in most relationships, it should not serve as an impediment to your taking care of yourself when you are being abused and exploited. Chances are good that your girlfriend will move on to someone else while you are still surveying the damage and trying to make sense of what has happened. It's a sad, ugly truth. Your disordered girlfriend has been benefitting from your desire to operate as an ethical, caring person while she has been unwilling or unable to operate on the same terms. Now, it's time to drop her out of the equation and redirect all of the attention, time, energy, and resources you have been devoting to her to the process of caring for your own precious life. The time has arrived for you to be your own best partner.

GETTING OUT

Too many of us know how to get into a relationship without having the skills to get out. Knowing when and how to get out of a destructive relationship may not only save your sanity; it may also save your life. The longer you stay in a relationship that is damaging to you and your well-being, the longer it will take for you to recover. Every day you spend in your toxic relationship is a day you subtract from the days you could be spending peacefully in your own company or enjoying a true partner with whom you can experience delight, security, and mutual care.

By now you know how you are hooked by a toxic relationship. In this chapter, we are going to explore a concept that may have your stomach in knots: getting out. This chapter offers strategies for getting out of a destructive relationship. There is an exit door. And just like the fire exit in theatres, it exists for the safety of everyone. Your leaving a destructive relationship benefits everyone involved --- you, the people who love you and worry about you, the people around you for whom you cannot be fully present because of the ways this relationship is damaging your heart, your health, and your creativity, and, ultimately, your girlfriend, whose toxic, dysfunctional behavior is enabled as you continue to allow her access to you.

You have come to this book because you are suffering. Like the women I interviewed for the book, your relationship with a personality disordered girlfriend is draining your life energy, your optimism, and your peace and well-being, possibly along with your health, your bank account, and your sense of safety and happiness. You may even have skipped right to this chapter in your search for a strategy to find some relief or to find some permission to leave because your girlfriend's successful installation of fear, obligation, and guilt in you prevents you from seeing clearly that leaving is a viable, desirable option.

If things were better, and you could rationally expect your girlfriend to make real, sustainable progress on the issues that allow her to feel okay about manipulating or deceiving you, exploiting your time and energy, or keeping you in a constant state of agitation, you wouldn't be here. The fact that someone pointed you toward this book or you found it on your own search for answers says that removing yourself from the path of destruction is likely going to be the most sane and loving thing you can do.

Ending relationships with women with personality disorders can be especially difficult. You may have reservations about leaving and struggle mightily with this decision. You may be very emotionally ready to leave, on the other hand, but find leaving difficult because you very reasonably expect the ending will be complex, messy, and involve a range of risks. In this chapter, I will talk with you about both the emotional and the logistical elements of deciding to end a relationship with a personality-disordered partner.

TRUST YOUR COMMITTEE

If you have been sharing with your friends what is happening in your relationship, they have no doubt been encouraging you, begging you, pressuring you to remove yourself from your toxic situation. Why? Because they hate seeing you suffer. They know that you deserve to be happy, and they believe, based on the evidence, that the relationship you are in will bring you unending heartache.

If you have not been clueing your friends and family in on how things are going in your relationship, if you have been withholding or managing the details of how your girlfriend treats you in order to avoid others' judgment, concern or intervention, you know in your heart that things are twisted. *Good, healthy relationships are relationships that you need not be ashamed of, embarrassed by, or afraid to reveal to others.*

It is important to distinguish between lesbians keeping relationships in the closet from fear of homophobic reactions and lesbians keeping the details of toxic relationships in the closet in order to protect an abusive partner. Healthy relationships are blessings to families and communities; they provide support, inspiration, and energizing to partners, as well as to the people around them. If your relationship is a concern to others, or if you are hiding its demoralizing or painful elements from others, it is time to free yourself (and your girlfriend) from this dynamic.

If your friends or family urge you to end the relationship, you must pay attention. The women I interviewed for this book frequently reported friends having an important impact on their decisions to end toxic relationships. Some reported friends inviting them to come to their homes to seek respite. Others reported that friends began to avoid them in order to steer clear of the poison:

She was toxic and she was mean to me. So they were just like, "we can't witness that shit." They said, "when she's gone, let me know and I will come over and have a beer with you.

They told me, "Call the cops." "Get an alarm system." "What are you doing?" "You've gotta get out. You've gotta get out." When two of my dearest, closest friends said, "I love you. I can't talk about this anymore. I support you, and you know how I feel about this situation, and I don't want to hear about her anymore until you do something about it." It worked. Two friends. Two friends had to say that to me—independently. Within a month, I ended it. I looked into an alarm system here. I cut her off. I told her no contact. I realized that I had stretched my friends' patience. And I knew that they were telling me what was good for me, and that they cared about me. I wasn't willing to lose my friends over a lunatic.

Friends sometimes have their own vested interests and judgments about each others' romantic involvements, and it makes sense to be thoughtful about whose advice you trust. However, if people in your girlfriend's life are pulling you aside and warning you away from her, or if your own friends are encouraging you to end your relationship, pay attention. Confronting a friend about her relationship choices is usually not done lightly, but the people who know you best and who have a history of treating you well and looking out for your best interests are stepping up to protect you. They will be present to help you put things back together when you decide it is time for you to exit.

WHY IS IT SO HARD TO SET THE WILD THINGS FREE?

On the surface, this would seem to be an easy decision: if the person you are involved with is cruel or behaves in ways that make you uncomfortable, it makes sense to drop them and not look back. Friends looking in on your relationship from the outside, and hearing about your girlfriend's deceptions, manipulations, or drama, quickly arrive at the rational recommendation to extricate yourself from the situation. Unfortunately, doing this can be far, far more difficult than it sounds, as anyone involved with a personality disordered person for any length of time knows. Why? Think about all of the forces that we have talked about so far that took you from "we just met" to "we are a couple" in very short order. If you simply were dating, it might be very possible to notice the warning signs early on, but the personality disordered person may have glommed onto you "like white on rice;" she may have put on an emotional full court press very early that tapped into your deep desire to find someone with whom to partner. She may have said the things you have been longing to hear. She may have listened to you attentively and romanced you ardently. She no doubt created the impression that she could deliver whatever means the most to you in a relationship. She may have pulled a bait-and-switch, offering a casual sexual encounter and then never leaving, holding you emotionally hostage until she lines up her next victim. So, you may have gotten in very deep very fast, which makes walking away more difficult than it would have been in the earlier stages of conventional dating.

Social psychologists have long understood that investments of time, money, and energy make people loyal to projects, institutions, or processes. We tend to value things and experiences more if we have worked for them or paid for them in some way. Old-school sorority and fraternity hazing worked based on this principle. Military boot camp often does the same. People in business and in the non-profit sector know that they can sometimes sell things that they couldn't give away. Community organizers have learned that charging a nominal fee for an event gives those who attend a greater sense of investment than simply putting an event on for free. In abusive or exploitive situations, people tend to become loyal to people who make them suffer, especially if they have invested in helping, supporting, or rescuing them. Sorority and fraternity hazing, military boot camp, and other rites of initiation that involve suffering count on it: once a person has gone through a certain amount of discomfort and suffering to become a member of the club, they often become fiercely loyal it and justify their mistreatment. Making a deposit on an apartment is similar; ostensibly, it holds the apartment, reserving it for you. Emotionally, the fact that you have made an investment increases the chances that you will actually take the place, even if you find someplace else easier and more appealing.

So, in your relationship with a disordered person, you have likely made significant investments of time and energy --- and these have been disproportionate to the investments made by your girlfriend. Because you have thought she was special, or especially in need, you have made these contributions to get into or stay in "her club." *Social psychology tells us that once we start investing, we keep investing. Your abusive girlfriend counts on this. And she counts on this standing in the way of your summoning up the energy to leave.*

More disturbing then the investments in abusive relationships creating affection and loyalty is the fact that people have a tendency to invest more and commit more *when*

134

a project is failing. It seems totally illogical, but you are probably engaged in this dramatic effort to save a sinking ship right now, or can see that you have done this in the past, much to the dismay of your friends, your therapist, and anybody who is hip to how your girlfriend treats you. Check out this summary of these kinds of dynamics from a 2007 article by Keiko Aoki, Yohsuke Ohtsubo, & Amnon Rapoport, an international team of social psychology researchers:

> When people invest resources in a project that turns out to be unsuccessful, they tend to commit to the failing project by making additional investments. Social psychologists have studied this tendency under the rubrics of sunk cost (Arkes & Blumer, 1985), entrapment (Rubin & Brockner, 1975), or escalation (Staw, 1976; Teger, 1980). For example, the sunk cost effect refers to "a greater tendency to continue an endeavor once an investment of money, effort, or time has been made" (Arkes & Blumer, 1985, p. 124). Two major factors have been identified as facilitating a commitment to a failing course of action: *prior investment* (e.g., Arkes & Blumer, 1985) and *personal responsibility* (e.g., Staw, 1976).

Prior investment and personal responsibility set people up for following possibly good small investments (exploring a relationship) with bad investments (wasting time, energy, and money on a relationship disaster). Remember that strong sense of responsibility and obligation that showed up in our list of "hooks" that keep lesbians snagged in unrewarding toxic relationships? It is easy to see, from the lens of these principles in social psychology, how decent, competent, and resourceful women get hooked into over-giving in relationships with personality disordered girlfriends who cannot reciprocate in degree or in kind.

I think our people think people are like slot machines. I've got so much invested ---I've got money, I've got time, I've got emotion --- this has got to pay off. Somewhere I am going to do something right; I'm gonna hit the right combination, and it will be okay. That's just wrong thinking. I know. So I just thought if I take care f the dogs; if I settle whatever with child custody...eventually it would be enough.

Your girlfriend may also be working something sociologists call "the principle of least interest," which also gets in the way of your leaving. The principle of least interest holds that *the person with the most power in a relationship is the person who has less interest and fewer investments.* When we sense that the other person is less interested, we typically step up our game.

In your case, if your narcissistic, borderline, histrionic, or sociopathic girlfriend has a tendency to back off, run cold, reverse course, incite your need to compete with other women for her attention, and not be present to your needs and desires, she inadvertently or intentionally manipulates you into staying connected through the principal of least interest. So, feeling responsible, you continue to give more to save failing projects because of your prior investments in them, along with the principle of least interest keep you hooked in, stuck, and desperate. The principle of least interest can move you into feeling desperate about saving a failing relationship; you may find yourself chasing after a girlfriend who is cheating on you because you yourself do not want to be rejected by someone who is so obviously bad news. Your previous investments, coupled with your sense of responsibility, lead you to invest even more when you begin to panic that you are looking at a disaster. Devoting more resources than you can afford to the project of saving the relationship partly explains how people end up broke, homeless, ill, addicted, isolated, unemployed, or left with not much more than a tragic tale to tell in the wake of toxic relationships with narcissists, sociopaths, and borderlines.

I think of the lesbian who left a terrific, secure job she loved and a home she owned in a desperate attempt to please a disordered girlfriend who pressured and manipulated her into moving to another part of the country despite her better judgment. Each effort to please and placate the girlfriend was met with the girlfriend's greater pressure for a more expensive or risky effort to maintain or improve the relationship. A couple of years later, she was bankrupt, foreclosed upon, without job security, in a part of the country where she had little community, and desperate to end her legal and financial entanglements with the girlfriend, who had pushed early in the relationship for them to go to Canada to be married. In this case, the partner's sense of responsibility and the tendency of people to invest greater resources in failing projects were successfully used against her by her sociopathic partner.

Small investments lead to larger investments; when you are dealing with personality disordered girlfriends those larger investments can lead to nightmare scenarios --- disasters that the disordered girlfriend has no interest in averting or mitigating. In fact, the narcissistic, sociopathic, or borderline girlfriend will use the disasters that result from your involvement with her as evidence that you are dysfunctional or crazy; she will announce that "she told you" to be more financially responsible and minimize the fact that she pressured you to leave your good job so she could live her dream.

Knowing about the principle of least interest, the tendency to be loyal to relationships for which we over-work and over-sacrifice and suffer, and the tendency for people in general to give more instead of to cut their losses when they are facing a losing battle, can allow you to think differently about why you are staying, what is preventing you from leaving, and how much responsibility (debt, risk, illness) you're taking on in the process.

WHAT'S LOVE GOT TO DO WITH IT?

When people ask you why you are having so much trouble ending a relationship with a woman who treats you badly, keeps you on edge, and distracts you from the broader goals in your life, you may tell them "because I love her." You may say that you are afraid that you won't have another chance at a relationship. You may find yourself saying "well, we had an okay week this week," expressing the hope that things could get better and be better on a consistent basis. Given the crash course in social psychology we've just had, I hope you are beginning to see that in the presence of a personality disorder, improvements are often only temporary and serve to keep you hanging in there one more week, month, or year. Love, although present, may be the least of the things standing in your way of getting yourself to higher, safer ground. In fact, I will argue next, if you really love her, you will set her free.

Real love and compassion fortify each other, and neither true love nor true compassion is weak, sappy, or indulgent. Love is not so much an emotion but a practice, a set of principles put into action. Allowing your disordered partner to behave in disordered ways, to treat you with disrespect, to speak abusively to you, and to treat you and your resources with disrespect not only exploits you: it enables her. If you stay with a partner who has a narcissistic, sociopathic, or borderline personality disorder and you feel responsible for her welfare get clear on this: her disorder will not improve if you continue to enable or reinforce it by staying in a toxic relationship with her. If you cannot bring yourself to end this relationship, yet, based on how bad it is for you, consider liberating her from it based on how bad it is for her. If you don't love yourself enough to liberate yourself, at least love her enough to set her free.

Many lesbians and queer women in relationships with narcissists, sociopaths, and borderlines want the answer to the questions they are asking to be anything but "end it." In fact, their questions often don't focus on what they need to do to take care of themselves but instead center on why this woman is so unpredictable, dramatic, and inconsistent in her stories; why she is, by turns, needy and distant; why she constantly accuses you of planning to leave her, even while she destroys your self-confidence and suggests you are not worth her time. Often, partners want the drama and deception and inequities to go away, and the relationship to be salvaged, with an emphasis on its good qualities. You may attribute your GF's crazy behavior to the ex- she blames it on, to various medical illnesses, and to the long established byproducts of trauma she reports in her childhood. You spend a lot of time and energy researching what might explain this brilliant, funny, charming, talented woman's unstable behavior and resist the encouragement of friends and family to end the relationship. Why? Because of the way the hooks have been attached.

While asking these questions keeps your mind occupied, it does little to give you any relief or to move your life forward. A more productive line of thinking is to ask: "What is the root of my suffering?" "What do I need to do to end my suffering?" "What are the barriers to my taking skillful action?" And "How can I eliminate those barriers?"

Imagine this: you are crossing the street and discover yourself in the path of an oncoming speeding car. Maybe the drivers' parents didn't teach her how to drive, but she has gotten behind the wheel anyway, thinking she will learn as she goes. She doesn't have the skills to protect you as she drives because she is so focused on her own experience. Maybe the driver feels angry at you, perhaps for your very presence in the street, and she feels justified in harming you. Maybe the driver is drunk and unable to control the car. She may not even notice that you are in front of her and will be harmed by her recklessness; you are, essentially, irrelevant, beyond her capacity to notice. Maybe the person is having stroke or heart attack, and losing control of the car as a result of her own crisis; she may or may not be aware of you and may or may not try to avoid doing damage to you.

No matter the explanation, you are in harm's way. In the end, when it comes to your safety and welfare, it doesn't matter why the driver is mowing you down with the car (except in court); what matters is that you are in harm's way. And your responsibility to yourself and the people who care for you is to move yourself out of the car's path. Standing in the road, contemplating why the driver drives as she does, or denying that no damage will be done because the driver doesn't intend to hurt you increases your risk. In relationships with people who are unkind, cruel, unstable, unpredictable, exploitive, abusive, or exhausting, no matter what explains their dysfunctions, you don't have to spend your life energy figuring out what why they treat you in harmful, hurtful, ways. What you have to do is keep yourself safe and well --- as anyone who truly loves you would want you to do. When you are in the path of a foreseeable disaster, get yourself out of the way as soon as possible.

HOW THE BEST THING FOR YOU IS ALSO THE BEST THING FOR HER

I would like to talk to you about why the most loving thing for you to do is end your relationship with your abusive girlfriend. Chances are that you aren't in a place yet to love yourself well enough to prioritize your own welfare, given how long you have been occupied with that of your disordered girlfriend. You may say that you know you need to get out. You may say you are desperate to get out, but that circumstances connected to legal issues, financial issues, career issues, or kid issues prevent you from acting. I understand that, having been there myself, so I would like to share with you a story that I find meaningful in thinking about the stakes involved with ending your relationship with a disordered person.

In her wonderful book *Loving-Kindness: The Revolutionary Art of Happiness,* the Buddhist teacher Sharon Salzberg (2011) tells a story about a man attempting to grab her from a rickshaw in which she and a friend were riding.

"I thought, 'Oh my God, this guy is going to drag me off and rape me and then he is going to kill me,'" she writes. Her friend intervened, pushing away the drunken assailant and urging the rickshaw driver away from the scene.

When Sharon got back to her teacher, Munindra, she told him this story.

Her teacher commented, "Oh, Sharon, with all the lovingkindness in your heart, you should have taken your umbrella and hit that man over the head with it!"

You may be surprised by this response by a peaceful meditation teacher. The message, however, is that you must ensure non-harm and well being of yourself as you ensure the non-harm and well-being of others. Allowing yourself to be abused is the same as passively standing by and allowing someone else to be harmed. You are as precious as every other living creature. And: allowing the attacker to harm you is a disservice to her or him. Imagine the negative karma she acquires each time she succeeds in hurting someone. The most compassionate thing we can do for someone harming us is to prevent him from doing harm.

141

Here's how Salzberg puts it:

> Sometimes we think that to develop an open heart, to be truly loving and compassionate, means that we need to be passive, to smile and let anyone do what they want with us. Yet this is not what is meant by compassion. Quite the contrary. Compassion is not at all weak. It is the strength that arises out of seeing the true suffering of the world. Compassion allows us to bear witness to that suffering, whether it is in ourselves or others, without fear; it allows us to name injustice without hesitation, and to act strongly, with all the skill at our disposal.

In your current situation, removing yourself from harm's way honors your own welfare. It also ends your participation in the patterns of exploitation, drama, parasitism, control, and abuse that characterize your disordered girlfriend's behavior.

BREAKING UP IS HARD TO DO (BUT NOT AS HARD AS STAYING)

Breaking up is one of those skills that some lesbians didn't have the chance to practice as teenagers, and as a result we may not end relationships as skillfully as possible, even under the best of circumstances.   It isn't easy to end relationships, and we may not have a lot of practice doing it cleanly, for all of the reasons we have already discussed throughout this book. We are, of course, not alone in this: folks in opposite sex relationships have plenty of drama as they go through break-ups and divorces. But opposite sex relationships are at least given a language of breaking up which includes songs, movies, novels, advice columns, and a wide range of other popular media. There are fewer models of lesbians walking away from toxic girlfriends and getting on with their happy lives.

Although endings in general can be sad and sometimes difficult, ending a relationship with a personality disordered person requires you to exercise special caution. Even if the relationship takes place long distance, the unpredictability of people with personality disorders means that you still need to bring a heightened awareness to the ending process.

Because even short "relationships" with disordered people can result in tumultuous endings, the ideal scenario is to figure out after a few dates if the person you are getting to know shows the warning signs of personality disordered behavior. The longer a relationship goes on and the more it assumes the trappings of coupledom, the more important it is that the break-up is handled with special thought and care.

BACKING OUT EARLY ON

Early on, when you make the observation that the person you are dating has significant traits of a personality disorder, you can end the relationship as you would a relationship with a non-disordered person. You have no obligation to explain your decision to stop dating the woman or to sugar coat things. The best strategy simply is to say: "I have realized that we are not a good match. I have decided not to continue to go out with you. I wish you all the best as you continue to look for a partner."

Resist the temptation to soften this message with anything that might give your date or girlfriend the false hope of reconciliation, such as reassuring her about her great qualities or suggesting that if the timing were different, you would be interested; these are not true in this situation.

It is important that the message be clean, clear, firm and without drama. Remember: ambiguity is the heart of drama and clarity is the heart of peace. Resist pressure to explain your decision. Share your decision in as level a way as possible, and avoid getting pulled into calls, texts, and e-mails from your girlfriend that are designed to rope you back into the dynamic you have already identified as unhealthy for you. Healthy people respect each other's boundaries. If your date or girlfriend protests your decision or uses a range of strategies to re-engage, it is a sign that you are correct in your assessment that this person is bad news for you.

People who are emotionally healthy and have good relationship skills know how to accept no for an answer. When you decide to end a relationship with a personality disordered person, even in the early stages, she may test your resolve in a number of ways, depending on the features of her personality. She could, for example, send you coy text messages asking you if you are sure about your decision and expressing regret, in a vague way, for her part in it. She could show up at your door with roses and pronouncements. She could turn on the charm. She could threaten suicide. She could behave as though nothing has happened. She could stalk and harass you, or engage in a smear campaign about you on social media.

How people with different personality disorders respond to break-ups varies to some extent with the disordered pattern and the traits within the pattern that are most prominent in the person. By the time you have found this book, you will likely have become pretty aware of the disordered responses that are most typical of your girlfriend. For example, has she broken up with you a number of times, only to pretend later that she didn't tell you she was through with you? If so, you can probably expect that she will try a number of times to test you or to reel you back in when you make it clear things are over.

Has your girlfriend proven herself a narcissistic or sociopathic bully? If so, it won't be surprising if she harasses you, bullies you, tries to enter your property without your knowledge or permission, vandalizes or destroys your possessions, or threatens to destroy your reputation or livelihood. She feels entitled to violate you in these ways, and needs to prove to you that she still has the upper hand, given how your ending the relationship has challenged her grandiose sense of self. Prepare yourself for the reality that she may make lots of drama with you and attempt to gain the sympathy of anyone who will listen to her account of how you wronged her by ending things.

All of these moves are designed to suck you back into the relationship, soothe her bruised ego, or both. If your girlfriend is a sociopath, this is about power. If your girlfriend is a narcissist, this is about her losing her narcissist supply. If your girlfriend has borderline traits, this is about her frantic effort to void abandonment. In all instances, it is about manipulating you in ways that have nothing to do with meeting your needs.

Below, I offer a set of re-engagement strategies that a personality disordered person may use in response to a break-up, Sometimes people call these "Hoover Maneuvers," to reference the Hoover vacuum cleaner and its reputation for having powerful abilities to suck things in. After each "Hoover" technique, I include my recommendation for how best to respond to these efforts on the part of your ex to re-engage your attention.

RESPONDING TO HOOVER MANEUVERS: DON'T GET SUCKED BACK IN

1. Maneuver: Suicide attempt, gesture, threat

Response: Call police; send them to girlfriend's location

2. Maneuver: Shows up at your door. Response: Don't answer

3. Maneuver: Calls. Response: Block number

4. Maneuver: E-mails. Response: Send e-mail to spam folder

5. Maneuver: Stalks home or work or social life. Response: Inform police; inform security at work; file for restraining order

6. Maneuver: Commits or threatens to commit violence against you, pets, property. Response: Call police; file for restraining order

7. Maneuver: Trashes you in public or on social media. Response: Consult with attorney; do not respond directly or wage a counter-response in public; arrange for attorney or police to contact her

8. Maneuver: Takes up with someone else. Response: Recognize the benefits of this; process the pain privately and with a therapist; do not contact new love interest

9. Maneuver: Disappears and/or does not participate in making arrangements to wrap up pragmatic details associated with ending the relationship. Response: Notify her in writing of how you plan to take care of things and then take action; engage as little as possible and only about pragmatic issues when she surfaces.

If you haven't been sharing an address or any joint acquisitions with your disordered girlfriend, things are somewhat simpler, although they still have plenty of potential for conflict, drama, and stress. Disordered people have engaged in the full spectrum of difficult behaviors even after the end of very short relationships. These behaviors include stalking, harassing by phone, mail, e-mail or text, waging character assassination campaigns, interfering with their former date's professional reputation, filing bogus police complaints or law suits, staging intensive reunification efforts, destroying or vandalizing property, harming animals, and perpetrating physical violence. I am sorry to say that it is the case, but personality disorders impair people's judgment, generosity, empathy, integrity, and information processing, all of which can result in a very bumpy ride through a break-up.

YOUR SAFETY FIRST

Despite the differences in "the flavors of crazy," you need to be very thoughtful about your personal safety, the safety of your pets and children, the safety of your property, and the safety of your finances. You also need to protect your personal and professional reputation. If you married this woman or own a home together, it is absolutely necessary that you involve a lawyer; if you don't have these legal ties, you may still want to consult a lawyer. You need to be aware of the complexities of your legal rights to the space you occupy, if your girlfriend has been living there with you, whether you own or rent. You need to understand your right to make claims on any joint property you may have acquired, especially big ticket items like homes, cars, and other forms of

If you are married, you need to know what right you have to your partner's retirement fund and property, and what rights she has to yours. You also need to figure out, if you are married, how to get a divorce. If there are children involved, you need to understand what your rights in them are and what hers are. You need to take all of these things into account when making an exit plan; the more information you have, the better you will be able to create some security for yourself when you decide to exit.

THE PAST AS A PREDICTOR OF THE FUTURE

You have been with this woman long enough to have a sense of her modus operandi, how she operates. Do you know how she has ended other relationships?

Amanda, for example, reported that her former girlfriend enjoyed using the element of surprise to disorient her partners during break-ups. Once, she moved out of a partner's home after a break up, called a charity, and arranged a pick-up of the furniture she left behind, including the bed. The charity knocked on the door and announced they had come for the scheduled pick-up, completely shocking the ex-partner, who was left without a bed to sleep in. This gave the sociopath immense pleasure. In a subsequent relationship, she exited by making a surprise break-up announcement to her partner while dropping her at an airport for a professional trip abroad. She had no apparent empathy for the woman, who needed to process this information in front of colleagues waiting for her at the airport, and no consideration of what it might be like to try to address the emotional and financial fallout of the breakup of a household that would be "cleaned out" while she was out of the country.

Given this history, Amanda successfully anticipated that ending her own relationship with this girlfriend would involve lead efforts by the ex to make her suffer, particularly in front of others, in an event that included the element of surprise. Such behavior is designed to give a narcissist a sense of superiority in a "Gotcha" moment. Use what you know about your personality disordered girlfriend's history and patterns to do what you can to protect yourself from the worst of her reactivity in her interactions with you.

No matter the specific personality disorder of your girlfriend, and no matter whether you live together or apart, here are some important issues that you need to address in your exit plan.

DEVELOPING AN EXIT STRATEGY

Decide for yourself how, when, and where to tell your girlfriend your decision and your plan for resolving any unresolved issues between the two of you. Although in healthy relationships in which emotional safety is present, having a direct, face-to-face conversation with a date, girlfriend, or partner about breaking up is responsible and caring, this may not be the best approach with girlfriends who have personality disorders. If you have observed your girlfriend repeatedly distorting reality for the benefit of her own ego or to manipulate others, you may wish to advise her in writing of your decision to end the relationship. You cannot control how she will present this to others, but you can control the language you use and the message you send. You are creating a record that may be useful to you later, if your girlfriend tries to gaslight you by accusing you of saying things that you did not, or if giving her notice of some elements of the ending becomes significant legally in the future.

Some women in your position have taken a less direct route by deciding that the best outcome for them would result from the girlfriend breaking up with them. One woman I interviewed, for example, used this strategy:

I realized that she was going to need to end it with me. Because if I ended it with her there would be another round of suicide threats. So she was going to have to end it with me, which she did. She broke up with me because she met somebody else, and it was the first time that I did not pursue it again. She started calling me again and would complain about the new person. When she started questioning my intentions [with someone else] she became very accusatory and mean and I decided I was not going to talk to her.

While this strategy worked for this lesbian, other partners report they have used all manner of strategies to maneuver the disordered girlfriend into breaking up with them without success. In general, I recommend making a careful, active plan that puts you back into the driver's seat of your own life. Your girlfriend may accuse you of trying to control her, or of being a bully, when, of course, she has been controlling and bullying you throughout the relationship. Your goal here is not to control her, but to be free of her control, and to once again become centered in and responsible for your own life.

If you live together, you will need a timeline for separating your possessions and moving to separate living spaces. If it's your property, and your girlfriend is a squatter, determine a date by when she needs to be out. If the home belongs to your girlfriend, make a plan for when you will move out and all of the steps that need to be coordinated to make that happen. If you are both on the deed or the lease, determine what your legal options are for terminating your mutual rights and obligations.

If you have been living together, or if she has had a key to your place, plan to change the locks as soon as possible, taking into account what you learn about your legal rights to do so. If you are moving to a new place, select it with your security in mind. If you have concerns about intrusive behavior on her part, you may wish to rent a post office box so that your physical address is less available to the public. Be mindful of how easy it is for people to find information online about your address and phone number, and take measures to protect your privacy.

If you have joint financial accounts, separate them as soon as you decide you will be exiting the relationship; end her access to your savings, checking, or credit card accounts. Terminate joint accounts.

Take her off of your health and life insurance policies or get yourself off of hers. When relationships that don't involve the dysfunctions associated with personality disorders end, and in legal divorces, these issues are often negotiated with thoughtfulness and care between partners or worked out by divorce attorneys. Unfortunately, in toxic relationships, informal agreements about these matters often fall apart when the disordered partner creates drama or difficulty or fails to uphold her end of the agreement. Do your best to make sure you are taking care of your own interests; do not act with a motive to harm the other person, but trust that she is more resourceful than you may have assumed, and that she will find a way to remedy any problem created by the end of the relationship.

Plan to terminate any domestic partnership you may have established. Take her name off of any accounts on which she may be a beneficiary.

Change the passwords on your e-mail addresses, Facebook accounts, and bank accounts, even if you believe your girlfriend doesn't know them or would never take advantage of them.

If you have joint property or possessions [vehicles, travel condos, campground sites, second homes or retreat spaces or land] consider whether you are willing to let these things go or how to assert your legal claims to them. If for some reason you have placed your assets in your girlfriend's name alone, be prepared to lose them or, with an attorney, explore what would be involved with recovering them or their value.

If you are in the midst of achieving an important life goal --- adopting children, finishing a degree, earning a promotion or landing your dream job, buying a home, undergoing a gender transition, attending to a dying or ill parent, launching your own business --- expect that your soon-to-be former partner will attempt to manipulate you into   sabotaging yourself. She will do this by creating some kind of drama at a critical point in the process. You must become exquisitely clear about your own commitment to your own goals and priorities, so that when the drama hits, you will be able to stay your own course.

DON'T BE SHOCKED BY A WORST-CASE ENDING (AWE)

You will need to have a plan of action, based on your priorities and your knowledge of your girlfriend, for an Absolute Worst-case Ending (AWE) scenario --- you know, the one in which your ex engages in some action that is reminiscent of the US effort to inflict "shock and awe" on its military enemies. Remember, you may be dealing with a chocolate-covered explosive device.

Imagine this as an AWE scenario: you come home to discover your space ransacked, your credit cards missing, your clothing and computer destroyed, suicide threats scrawled on your walls, your animal friend hiding in the closet, and the police waiting for you. Your ex has reported to the police that you have created this chaos, are suicidal, and should be committed. She has told them she is going into hiding because she is afraid of you. It is the night before you are supposed to go to court to finalize the adoption of your foster child, or defend your dissertation, or to start a new job, which, of course, she knows. In this AWE scenario, what will you do that will allow you to prevail in taking care of your life and your goals? How would you respond to the police? How would you deal with the missing credit cards? How would you deal with the mess? Where would you spend the night? What are the most important things for you to do to make sure you are where you need to be in the morning? And what kinds of action would you take to respond to your ex-girlfriend, and on what timeline? Plan and prepare to address this extreme scenario, or another that you devise that is more relevant to you, and you will be prepared for nearly anything that happens.

GOODBYE GRRRL

I share these strategies not to scare you, but to prepare you. My hope is that through careful preparation for ending a toxic relationship, you will be able to take the next steps to reduce the drama in your life and to respond with clarity and calm if there are a few explosions over the course of the ending process. The fact that there is some risk of this again tells you how toxic your relationship has become and how important it is for your health and happiness that you get out.

Years ago, I had the benefit of working for the Rape Education and Prevention Program at Ohio State University. We provided not only education about sexual assault prevention, but also self-defense classes designed to give women (and, eventually, gay men) practical self-defense skills. Something I learned from the amazing women who trained me to teach self- defense is how powerful it can be to respond to our own fears with mental rehearsal.

For example, if you fear your ex-girlfriend will show up at your workplace and make a scene, you could simply allow that image to replay itself again and again in your mind, making you increasingly anxious. By alternative, using this technique, you could allow the image to come up and then move forward into images of how you could respond in this situation from a centered and creative space. If your ex-girlfriend shows up at your workplace to make a scene, imagine refusing to see her when someone tells you she is there. Or imagine coming into the lobby and repeating only "you need to leave now." Or imagine stepping away from her and calmly calling security. Or imagine noticing her in the parking lot, turning, and going inside to report her trespassing to police. Imagine allowing your girlfriend to rant and rave while you calmly observe, without reactivity or fear, recognizing that her behavior is only a reflection on her. There are many ways you could respond effectively to a situation like this. By meeting the anxious scenarios that come up as you plan to exit, you put your fears and anxieties into their proper proportions --- and you mentally prepare for the worst case scenario, which is often far worse than the worst case reality.

If you're fortunate, the greatest barrier to leaving is your own misplaced sense of responsibility or loyalty or hope. Your situation may be far more complex, however, and involve many practical concerns. Sometimes, in order to end toxic relationships that were literally destroying their health along with their happiness, partners of narcissists, borderlines, and sociopaths have chosen to sign over homes, allow foreclosure, file for bankruptcy, and risk their careers as a result of these injuries to their financial histories. These are extremely difficult experiences. However, making these moves, when necessary, has also saved women's lives, allowed them to restore their health, and have returned peace to their daily existence.

In addition, each of these solutions creates temporary circumstantial challenges from which people regularly recover. New jobs can be found; credit ratings can be restored; even people who have had homes foreclosed upon or filed for bankruptcy have restored their credit scores and returned to home ownership. I can comfortably argue that it is far easier to resolve the problems created by each of these sometimes necessary moves than it would be for you to create a loving, trustworthy, productive, collaborative partnership with integrity with a girlfriend who regularly violates your trust, manipulates you, exploits you, or explodes at you. Each day you stay in a toxic situation, your life accumulates more poison. The more poison that accumulates in your system, the higher your chances of becoming seriously ill and the more time you will need to fully recover. Each day you make progress on removing yourself from the toxic environment, you create more space in your life for peace, rest, and joy. The path out sometimes is a long one, and you are already tired. The sooner you start on your way, the sooner you will begin to recover, and the sooner you will reach your happy destination.

BECOMING YOUR OWN ALLY AND ADVOCATE

We have explored how, in combination with your personal hooks and intermittent reinforcement, the principle of least interest and sunk costs may keep you attached to a relationship that is unrewarding and that demands far more of you than it returns to you. We have acknowledged that even though there is hope for people with disordered personality patterns to heal and become more functional, this only happens when the person is deeply committed to change *and* is connected to a skilled therapist who doesn't reinforce her narcissistic, anti-social, or borderline patterns. The fact that your girlfriend is still behaving in ways that leave you feeling exploited, betrayed, invisible, edgy, exhausted, anxious, fearful, trapped, and unappreciated tells us that she is not getting the help she actually needs or engaging in a change process that will result in her becoming the partner you deserve. In the absence of her commitment to change and her lack of insight or concern for how her behavior affects you, changes for improving your circumstances are in your hands.

While the drama in your relationship may be about her, the relationship continuing is about you. You may have been victimized in this relationship, but now you need to move into the power position in your own life. Doing so will not only be beneficial to you but also to your girlfriend, because it does her the favor of getting one of her victims --- you--- out of harm's way and gives her the opportunity to take responsibility for her own life.

It is true that ending a relationship with someone with a disordered personality can be difficult. It involves not only the emotional risk of standing up for yourself, counting on yourself, and protecting yourself, but very practical risks related to retaliation and sabotage on your ex's part. The fact that you know there are such risks involved tells us that this relationship is toxic; break-ups may be sad, but they do not have to involve drama, hostility, and turmoil. Given that there are very real risks to your welfare and happiness in an ending with a personality disordered girlfriend, we also reviewed a number of issues to for you to consider as you plan to exit, in an effort to minimize the emotional, social, financial, and professional toll of the break-up on you.

Relationships with personality disordered people who are not committed to their recovery can be nightmarish. Break-ups often have dynamics that mirror those of relationships [if a person is fair and generous with you in a relationship, she will usually be fair and generous with you in a break-up, and the inverse is true here]. Depending on the details of the relationship, getting out or cleaning up the damage after you get out may take some time. The sooner you begin to prepare your exit, the sooner you can begin to set yourself free, and the sooner you will be able to create a life that is more consistent with your values, dreams, integrity, and commitments.

RECOVERY

Your relationship isn't helping you greet the world with joy and anticipation every morning. As valiantly as you have dedicated time, money, energy, therapy, and other resources to this failing project, it isn't turning itself around. Sooner or later, if you can have some vision of yourself living a happier life, you will make the decision to do what now appears as the most difficult thing to do: move on.

As we have seen from the principles of social psychology, the sooner you can put the brakes on your tendency to over-give and over-function, the sooner you can cut your losses and move on with the next phase of your life. You now have a deeper understanding about your vulnerability to the intermittent reinforcement, the sunk costs, the lesbian population pressure, and your own personal hooks as well as a deeper understanding of how difficult it is for people to change fundamental elements of their personalities. With this understanding and awareness, you will be able to free yourself from the toxic relationship in which you have been suffering. You can find the wisdom and strength to move on to the next phase of your life, which promises to be happier, healthier, and more peaceful.

ENDINGS

When relationships end in clean ways, people pick themselves up, dust themselves off, and move on relatively quickly. Relationships with people with borderline, narcissistic, or sociopathic patterns, however, generally don't allow for clean endings. As you know, such relationships are complicated, confusing, addictive, and highly problematic; and endings for these relationships can have the same qualities --- they can be dramatic, difficult, expensive, and, unfortunately, prolonged---just as the relationships were. As a result, recovering from them requires more than the ordinary natural closure that takes place in non-toxic relationships.

Recovering from such relationships is more like recovering from the trauma people experience in natural disasters, wars, or hostage situations. Many former partners report symptoms of Post-Traumatic Stress Disorder. As time goes on and you begin to feel more centered, more yourself, and more clear-headed, you will likely look back on your experiences in this toxic relationship and be amazed at what you tolerated. But you first need to get distance between yourself and the relationship. As you begin to heal, you will also become more aware of the ways this relationship has affected you and your life. Time and distance will allow you to make meaning of your experience of your own heart, wisdom, and resilience as you have come to understand them through the relationship you have survived.

In this chapter, I offer a variety of recommendations to support you in your process of recovery from a crazy-making relationship.

ADD A COUNSELOR TO YOUR TEAM

I cover here many of the self-care and recovery practices that a good therapist would encourage you to explore. However you may decide that you would benefit from therapeutic support, especially as you prepare to exit, begin to execute your exit plans, and deal with any drama that ensues, and begin the recovery process. Counseling, coaching, or therapy can provide you a secure and confidential space to speak your truth in the midst of the crazy dynamics of a relationship with a personality disordered person, have your perceptions validated or challenged, as needed, and receive competent coaching about how to move forward.

When you are looking for a therapist, it may be beneficial to work with someone who has some familiarity with personality disorders and some experience treating trauma. A therapist with these kinds of backgrounds will not be shocked or surprised by the stories you may tell her about what has been going on in your relationship and how difficult it has been to leave. She will also be able to assess you for signs of post traumatic stress, and to treat you appropriately for its symptoms, along with the mental health challenges clinicians more often see, such as depression and anxiety.

Although you may not be able to locate a lesbian or LGBTQ practitioner, or may not wish to work with one, it does make sense to ask any prospective therapist if he or she is comfortable working with lesbian or otherwise queer-identified clients and how much familiarity he or she has with LGBT communities and concerns. If you are living in a small town or are for other reasons especially concerned about seeing a therapist who may be connected to your professional or social circle, consider finding a counselor in a nearby town or locating someone who does work virtually.

Therapy is not for everyone and women do recover without the benefit of a therapist's support. Whether or not you seek out a counselor, you can use this chapter as a recovery tool and as a guide to some of the best practices that a therapist would support you in as you end and recover from your toxic relationship. These practices will help you to recover more quickly and effectively, and will allow you to put this difficult relationship behind you as fast and firmly as possible w/o relapsing --- either with your disordered ex or with someone similar who will sense your neediness and vulnerability in the aftermath of this emotional disaster.

MEETING SELF-JUDGMENT WITH COMPASSION

It is very common to feel a lot of self-judgment in the wake of a disastrous relationship. In truly intimate relationships ---both friendships and partnerships--- we assume that what the people close to us tell us is true, and that what we are seeing is real.

In relationships with people who have personality disorders, there often are elements of deception and manipulation. Some of these may have been significant in your decision to end the relationship. Unfortunately, as you are processing the relationship in its aftermath, new information may come your way that deepens your understanding of how much may have been happening beyond your conscious awareness. Your ex may have been having affairs or playing you for money for "essentials" that went instead to indulgent luxuries; she may have been telling you she was too disabled to work while she was making plans with friends to take a long excursion. She may have been blowing off classes and failing to finish graduation requirements; when you thought she was at school, she was instead drinking with friends on a daily basis. You may discover that the house she told you she owned is actually owned by her ex, or that the "roommate" with whom she lives didn't know that the two of them were no longer a couple.

When this information comes to light, it is common not only to feel a wide range of complex emotions toward your disordered ex, but also some complex emotions directed toward yourself: shame, embarrassment, judgments about how you could be conned, duped, and played, and despondency about ever having the skills to select a good partner or to be chosen by someone who will cherish you.

When these feelings come up, they can set into motion a cascade of further self-judgment. Now, in addition to feeling distressed about what happened in such a difficult relationship, you may be distressed about your own participation, and then about how harsh you are being with yourself about that. It can be helpful to consider these thoughts and feelings might be thought of as parts of yourself that are trying to be helpful: harsh as they are, their goal is to protect you, educate you, and help you to avoid similar decisions in the future (trust me: the universe will provide you opportunities in the form of other women to test if you have learned the lessons it offered through this relationship). So: the intentions of these judgmental voices or damning thinking ultimately may be to protect you, but their harshness does not move you forward. You might respond to these thoughts not by validating them but by recognizing their intention to protect you, and then assuring yourself that you are learning from your situation and expect to be able to protect yourself better in the future.

If you can be gentle with the self-judging thoughts, move on to offering yourself some compassion for your situation. Understand that you are not alone in having gotten involved with a person who has a personality disorder; indeed, part of the person's disorder involves enticing people who are stable, generous, hard-working, and highly motivated into relationships with her. People with personality disorders can be experienced as emotional vampires; they feed on the energetic life blood of others. If your best friend came to you and reported that someone had berated her, stolen her wallet, and kicked her, would you tell her she was stupid for having allowed that to happen? Would you yell at her for being victimized? Or would you tend to her wounds, help her protect her identification and credit cards, and give her a hug, all while recognizing that she is a competent and caring human being? I am betting you would use the latter approach with your friend, and this is the approach that will likely be most beneficial to you as you patch yourself up while you process the end of the relationship and any new information that comes to light that deepens your awareness of ways you have been conned.

At some point you can also have compassion for your ex-girlfriend. To recognize that she is disordered is to recognize the tragedy of who she is: someone with immense capacities or potential, someone blessed with talents and gifts and attractive qualities, someone to whom others are attracted --- whose personality has been twisted so deeply that she cannot function effectively as a partner.

In time and through distancing yourself, compassion will come. Remember that to practice compassion is not the same as giving someone "a pass" for their hurtful behaviors. You can practice compassion by *not supporting* the dysfunctional behaviors or making yourself available as the object of someone's exploitation. Compassion is not indulgence or mindless sympathy; it is kindness coupled with right action; it is love big enough to stop grasping and wise enough to do whatever is necessary to support a person being her best self, even when that means removing ourselves from her orbit.

Remember this: love can be unconditional; participation in a relationship always has strings. You can love your ex from a distance, where it is safer for you and safer for her, no matter how much she may argue the contrary or act out as a result of your reclaiming your peace and centeredness. With compassion as a foundation you can move on to some very pragmatic practices that will accelerate your recovery. One of the most important of these is "no contact."

NO CONTACT

"No contact" means that you should have no contact with your ex-girlfriend.

Period.

This can be very difficult advice to hear, and difficult to enact. This can especially be the case for lesbians because of a long cultural tradition of continuing to have friendships with exes and concerns about over-lapping social networks within small communities. Nonetheless, the sooner you can achieve no contact, the more you can accelerate your recovery process.

Your relationship may have felt like you were in the throes of an addiction. Ending this relationship may look and feel a lot like ending a relationship with alcohol or drugs or some other addictive substance. All addictive substances change our brain chemistry to keep us coming back for more. When we try to stop using these substances, our brains (and other organs) go through withdrawal, and we can become very uncomfortable. Unfortunately, the quick fix for this discomfort is a reintroduction of the substance into our system. This gives us some relief, but it undermines our effort to stop using and takes us back to square one when we try to end the addiction again. The longer you have no contact with your ex, the more comfortable you will become with being clear of her. When you have a set-back, you undermine your emotional freedom and welfare.

So, when you have squared away as many details as possible related to ending your relationship with this woman, you need to move into the No Contact Zone. Ideally, this means, simply and completely, that you have no contact of any kind for any reason with your ex. This will provide you with some relief; it may also provide you with some anxiety, especially if you are now yourself "addicted" to the push-me/pull-you patterns in her behavior. That is, you may enter no contact but still be on edge about whether she will call--- or wonder if you have been too harsh, or whether you should call her, etc. As with substance withdrawal, this can be very uncomfortable. If it is, you can say to yourself, "this is like substance withdrawal. I am very uncomfortable. I wouldn't want to have to do this again. This discomfort will pass, and soon I will feel more comfortable and be free of my feelings of addiction toward my ex." *The longer you can live with the discomfort, the sooner you will move into a richer recovery from this toxic relationship.*

"No contact" is in some ways a misnomer. It implies that the only behavior that you need to avoid is talking with, e-mailing, texting, or meeting your ex-GF. As you well know, in the information society it is possible for us to have access to information *about* people without directly interacting with them. More than one of my clients recovering from a toxic relationship with a person with a personality disorder has been officially in the "No Contact Zone" when she decided to check out her ex-GF's Facebook page or website or blog; when this happens, the recovering person always discovers that she has just chosen to stir her own hornet's nest of unpleasant emotions. As a result of exposing herself to information about her ex, she experiences a set-back in establishing her own peace and quiet, and also has to deal with the knowledge that trolling her ex's Facebook page for information is intrusive, inappropriate behavior on her behalf --- not far from the behavior of her disordered ex.

So, no contact means both no contact and no exposure.

Set up your e-mail so that hers goes in your spam box; un-friend and block her on Facebook, or take yourself off of Facebook altogether; do not answer calls or texts or e-mails from her, in the purest form of no-contact. Remember how reinforcement works. Your consistency here is key to really establishing that this relationship is over.

I recognize that not everyone is in a situation that allows for absolute no contact; if you are co-parenting children for example, there will need to be some contact around logistics, but the less the better, especially because whatever you say could come back to you in court if the two of you end up there. As I noted in Chapter 5, if your relationship involved children, joint ownership of homes or businesses, or other legal complications, it is best to involve legal counsel, if at all possible. If you are co-parenting children with a woman with a personality disorder, it also makes sense to explore the kinds of support children will need in order to promote their emotional and physical health in the aftermath of your ending your relationship. If you are not the custodial parent and have no legal rights to the children, even if you have been parenting them, prepare for your ex to try to use the children as pawns or bargaining chips with you, and do your best to prevent this from happening, even if it means walking away --- which can be very difficult, but which models for the children the truth that right action sometimes involves removing yourself from a toxic situation.

If you believe the children are being abused in the home of their personality disordered parent, report this to child welfare authorities. If access to the children is beyond your control, do your best to let the children know that your exit is not about them, and that when they are of age, you will be happy for them to find you. Even if kids and property are not in the picture, there are many issues that initially you will feel require contact ---concert tickets, the pets, who gets the housewarming presents, etc. Most of these should have been addressed in your initial thinking about and communication over splitting up. If they were not, consider whether these issues really require contact, or whether you are using them as an excuse to contact your ex --- or vice versa.

WHAT SHOULD YOU DO IF YOUR EX CONTACTS YOU?

If your ex contacts you, do not respond right away; this just reinforces her contacting you and signals that you remain attentive and responsive. Decide if the issue has any real impact on the big picture of your life.

If your partner contacts you about some crucial unresolved business, respond as minimally as possible, as you might with a formal business associate. Remember, her sense of urgency no longer dictates your reality. You are unhooking yourself for her timing, her pace, and her needs. Give yourself breathing room to consider if, how, and when you want to respond. "I got your message" is a great phrase to use. If the person becomes demanding or bullying by phone, text, e-mail, or through social media there is never, ever a reason to respond directly. If the content of her messages is threatening or harassing, contact police and /or your lawyer; they can deal with her directly and effectively. Do not inconvenience yourself in the face of her demands; you have done that for too long.

If it is absolutely necessary to your own welfare to respond, do give yourself plenty of room to contemplate how to address her. You may want to go to a friend or therapist first to explore whether responding is truly necessary and, if so, the most effective and limited way to do so. You nearly always benefit by slowing things down in these circumstances. If nobody is bleeding, it is not an emergency.

If your ex threatens suicide, call the police and report the threat.

Never respond directly to harassment by your ex unless you are at risk of physical harm. And if you are being harassed, call the police. In sum: make a commitment to have two feet in the no contact zone; do not accept information about your ex from friends unless it pertains to your safety or welfare; do not creep her Facebook page or lurk around her website or blog; do not stretch beyond the boundaries of the No Contact Zone unless truly necessary, and then communicate in ways that are clear and as little reinforcing as possible.

Do behave honorably. If you owe her money, make arrangements to re-pay it and follow through with integrity; if you have her possessions, return them. Again, this should be part of the exit plan details that you considered in Chapter 4. Even though it is highly unlikely that your ex will exercise responsibility, integrity, respect, or fairness with you in your break-up, your conscience will thank you for behaving honorably. Comporting yourself this way will allow you to move on with your life and into another relationship without guilt, shame, or the ties of unfinished business. If your ex owes you money that she refuses to pay, make empowered choices about responding through legal action or cutting your losses. She must live with that knowledge, the weight of its karmic debt, and whatever consequences will come her way as a result of her abusive behavior. Find ways of recovering what she has taken from you that allow your conscience to remain intact.

THE LIMITS OF FRIENDSHIP

A concern that lesbians entering the No Contact Zone sometimes have is this: it violates the cultural tradition of lesbians remaining friends with their exes. This is about as well institutionalized in the culture as the third-date U-Haul scenario. I even saw a button at my local feminist bookstore that proclaimed "an army of ex-lovers cannot fail!" As lesbians, however, we also know that it is appropriate to think critically about cultural traditions, and this is one worth evaluating carefully. Some relationships end in such ways that both parties would like to remain/become friends after the romance or partnership ends. In other circumstances, however, it is perfectly appropriate to do what is more common in the heterosexual population: walk away (or back away slowly) and don't look back. If you bump into each other somewhere, nod or say hello, or have a brief conversation, depending on the circumstances, and keep on moving. A key point to remember is that in order to be friends later, you would need to be friends now. You are ending this relationship because you cannot trust this woman to take you into account or treat you respectfully. Authentic friendship is a basis of all healthy relationships. The basis of this relationship was never, ever a solid friendship, so there is nothing but prolonged pain to be gained by attempting to cultivate a friendship in the aftermath of the failed romance.

Population pressure and lesbian culture be damned. You need as much distance from this woman as possible.

EXQUISITE SELF CARE

You likely feel exhausted. You may even be sleep deprived. You are likely to be pretty uncomfortable in the No Contact Zone for a good (or bad) stretch of time, as you get a sense of how your ex is responding to the break up, deal

170

with whatever drama she tries to engage you in, or wonder what she might be up to in terms of retaliation. You may have been on high alert for a very long time, listening to Will Robinson's Robot screeching "WARNING! DANGER!" while trying to look and act normal and make things somehow functional with your girlfriend. It is going to take your nervous system quite a while to calm down. If your GF was one of those who likes to wake people up to fight and argue in the middle of the night, or who engages in such risky late night activity that you found yourself chronically worried about whether she was in a ditch somewhere, you are likely sleep deprived. As you become more comfortable in the No Contact Zone, and are confident in your home's security, one important thing you can do for yourself is prioritize sleep. For Annie, it was a critical part of the early phase of the break-up:

> *Immediately it was very sad. But it was Immediate relief, and also immediate safety feeling in my house again. Immediate peace. I could see it reflected in my animals. My dog, she would leave the room and go to the basement when something started between us. Sometimes I wouldn't even realize we were starting to escalate and until I saw her leave. She was like the Geiger counter. I was getting so conditioned I wasn't able to recognize what was going on. I wanted to be in the house and I didn't have to shut the bedroom door.*

A return to regular sleep will have many benefits to you as you enter recovery from your toxic relationship. Adequate sleep improves our health, our ability to process information, and our decision-making. It reduces the risk of heart attack, allows us to regulate weight better, and promotes better hormonal regulation in our bodies. Beyond this, sleep allows our brains an opportunity to integrate information in helpful ways, to process disturbing events, and to access our creativity and resilience. Your ex-partner may have explicitly used sleep deprivation as a strategy to keep you off center. Others contribute to sleep deprivation by causing drama when things are peaceful at night or through their own dysregulated habits or irresponsible habits. It is always a very good sign of recovery when one of my clients comes in --- often six months or a year after a rollercoaster relationship has ended ---and says "I am finally getting some decent sleep." If you feel the need right now to sleep more or even to go someplace other than home because you are too edgy to sleep there, take those impulses seriously. Your body is speaking, and it will reward you for listening.

While sleep is crucial as part of your exquisite self-care recovery package, other strategies for restoring balance to your body after what has essentially been a long siege of stress can include body work and energy medicine. Body work and energy medicine include massage, healing touch, acupuncture, reiki, neuromuscular therapy, Emotional Freedom Technique tapping and a number of other modalities designed to help your body and its energy systems return to balance. The experience of these treatments generally involves relaxing in a calming space where touch or energy work has clear healing intentions in the context of appropriate boundaries; in addition to helping your body begin to marshal its natural processes of restoration and recovery, these healing modalities offer you therapeutic touch in environments that should be free of stress, tension, and drama – a good antidote to the trials you have recently survived.

Yoga, historically, is a spiritually oriented mind-body practice designed to help its practitioners develop mind-body consciousness and wisdom. Incorporating yoga into your recovery practices can help you more deeply be in touch with your embodied experience during this transitional time. Like body work and other forms of energy medicine, yoga soothes the central nervous system and promotes balanced health. It also offers you a way to build both flexibility and strength, to practice observing your own limits, and to experience the difference between the feeling of expanding your capacity for healthy reasons and pushing yourself further than appropriate, an issue that you may have observed in yourself during your relationship. Yoga classes provide opportunities to receive the direct support and guidance of teachers and to meet other people developing commitments to health and wellness, but it is also possible to practice yoga in your living room, guided by books, DVD's, and YouTube videos. Don't let concerns about size or fitness deter you from trying this. Many places offer classes specially designed for larger bodies; despite the stereotype of skinny girls in spandex being the only people who practice yoga, yoga really is for everyone.

Like yoga, meditation is an ancient and versatile spiritual self-care practice that has many benefits both for those who practice it and for the world around us. You don't need to be a Buddhist to learn to meditate, although meditation is a well established practice in Buddhism. Meditation allows us to attune ourselves to our breathing, to calm our central nervous systems, to attend to what is happening in the present moment, and to slow down inside of external circumstances that may feel like tornados of drama. You don't need special equipment to do meditation, and, like prayer, meditation can be done anywhere --- at home, in your office, in an MRI machine, before an encounter with someone in whose presence you feel stressed.

There are many, many variations on meditation, many kinds of meditation, and many structured, formalized meditation practices. You can find basic introductions to its practices under "meditation" and "mindfulness practices" online and begin to integrate these into your daily self-care routine.

In a recent *Insights on the Edge* interview published by **Sounds True** (2013), host Tami Simon spoke with Dr. Kelly

McGonigal, a Stanford University health psychologist who integrates psychology, neuroscience, and medicine with the practices of mindfulness and compassion in her work about how to use meditation to strengthen your vision of your own best life. Dr. McGonigal described one meditation practice designed to move you toward clarifying your heartfelt desires and values, and strengthening your resolve to make decisions centered on them:

> One of the practices that I teach is a meditation practice that comes from the yoga tradition in which you go into a state of mindfulness, and from that state of mindfulness and awareness, you ask yourself questions about what it is you really want. You begin to put that into language. And you begin to put that into sensory images, what it feels like in your body, both what the longing or the heartfelt desire feels like in your body, and actually make a vow to yourself that you would like to make choices in your life that are consistent with that heartfelt desire and with that core value. And of course, you can do this not in meditation. But meditation seems to be a really powerful place to do it because it's allowing you both greater insight into your motivations so that you're less likely to be distracted by desires that actually create more suffering—and it also seems to be a good state of mind to really plant the seeds for future action. (Sounds True, 2013)

As you recover from your toxic relationship, it is vital for you to continue to cultivate a vision of the life you want to have now. You can use this meditation practice and many others to become clearer about what you want and who you want to be, to reduce your emotional reactivity to the past and move beyond it, and to restore balance, harmony, and delight to your life.

Staying active, too, can have miraculous benefits to you as you begin to reclaim your life. Whether exercising alone or with friends, by gentle walking or vigorous, competitive activity, exercise can increase your feel-good endorphins and bathe your brain in serotonin, both of which will help you ease any depressive symptoms you may have been struggling with in your relationship or following its ending. Exercise can also raise your sense of self-esteem as you feel better and look better, promote rest and relaxation, release pent up emotions, and give your body the symbolic message that "I'm not stuck anymore; I am moving forward."

Your social life may have become constricted during your toxic relationship. Maybe your controlling partner pressured you into seeing less of your friends or some friends have distanced themselves out of discomfort with the narcissistic, borderline, or anti-social behaviors of the woman with whom you have been involved. Sometimes friends believe that if they withdraw support from you while you are in an abusive relationship, you will drop the relationship in order to retain the friendship --- a strategy that has mixed results. Maybe your social world has become constricted because you have become too depressed and exhausted to keep up your friendships. You may have been over-working to support your exploitive partner or avoiding her friends so that they don't know what kind of difficulty you are experiencing. If your social world has atrophied as a result of your toxic relationship, an essential part of your recovery.

How you go about re-establishing a normal social life will vary, depending on who you are and what brings you pleasure. It may involve calling up old friends to re-establish your relationships with them. It may include making new connections or deepening connections with acquaintances that you have wished to know better. Be conscious about the people with whom you spend time and the quality of their partnerships and romantic relationships; being around people who are functional, mature, responsible, and able to reciprocate in their relationships will help to re-orient you to what "normal" looks like as you move away from a frame of reference that many people I talk with refer to as "Crazyland." If you are completely unsure how to start to establish a healthy social life, consider volunteering for an organization that does work you admire. You will add meaning to your life, expand your social world, and experience appreciation for your effort, time, and good intentions. Make a commitment not to date until the dust has settled on this toxic relationship and you feel emotionally free and available.

PRACTICE TRANSFORMATIONAL MAGIC

As you recover, there will likely be relationship loose ends and things that need to be addressed. Maybe you have moved and discovered something of hers packed into one of your boxes. Maybe she's moved and you discover that random things that were hers are still in the back of your closet. Maybe she has intentionally dumped things she doesn't want in your basement, leaving you to clean up yet another of her messes. Maybe after you tell her you are finally and truly done she leaves sends gifts to your home. What are you going to do with the material remnants of your relationship with someone who treated you very badly?

You are going to get rid of them.

"No contact" has some material conditions, and these include getting rid of things that belong to your ex, things that she gave you---if she gave you anything—and things that remind you of her. This is important for you energetically and emotionally because it helps the wounds to close by eliminating daily reminders of the relationship and it reduces your material and energetic ties to your ex.

I encourage you to dispose of these objects in ways that are not destructive to the objects or to your sense of your own integrity. We are not talking about your ex's family china, which you may need to return to her, or the bed she left in your basement, unless you have given her fair warning, to be clear --- these should have been taken care of in the big sorting. We are talking about the sweatshirt, the ring, the phone charger, the half bottle of shampoo, the chair that she decided not to move. You may have some impulses that make you want to burn her sweatshirt, cut up her phone charger, or trash her chair. The momentary gratification you may get from acting out in these ways pales in comparison to the long-term gratification you will receive from taking the high road. Throw out the shampoo, sure. No Contact means not smelling her scent in the bottle before you do. But donate the sweatshirt and the phone charger, give the chair to a college kid setting up her first apartment, and donate the ring to a non-profit's annual silent auction, where its energy can be transformed into good works in your community. The more creatively you dispose of this leftover stuff so that it benefits others the happier you will be.

FINDING YOUR OWN SWEET SPOTS AND CENTERS OF JOY

With this toxic relationship in your life, you have likely been distracted from sources of sweetness and pleasure in your life. Find your way back to the well and begin anew to water the seeds of happiness in yourself. For some, this may come in the form of travel or adventure. For some, it takes the shape of nurturing yourself and others through cooking. You may want to repaint your bedroom or renew your relationship with your garden, or begin a practice of dancing in your living room with friends every Friday night. You may find your heart opening to the goodness of life anew as you give yourself the time and space simply to watch sunsets or sunrises. Play with babies. Take long baths. Read books that inspire you. Sing with friends. Fill your home with music. Take long bike rides through beautiful terrain. Find the centers of sweetness and joy in your life and visit them more and more often. They've been waiting for your return.

MOVING BEYOND CRISIS MODE

As you work on exiting and recovering, each day is a day you are freer. If you have been in a toxic relationship for any length of time and are now exiting, much of your energy will be occupied for awhile by the crisis that breaking up may precipitate. You may be juggling the details of the financial fallout, moving, legal hassles, protecting your job, child custody, and personal safety. This can be overwhelming, which is why it's important to *think carefully about your exit plan,* prepare for A Worst-case Exit scenario unfolding, and build as much self-care as possible into your life, day by day. However challenging this is, trust that it will come to an end. Begin to contemplate goals for the far side of the exit crisis. It is important for you to continue to cultivate an even clearer vision of what you want your life to look like and how you can make that possible as the dust of this relationship settles. Life will go on, and it will go on without the crazy drama and emotional neglect or abuse that has been occupying so much of your head and heart.

You may find that this relationship, built though it was on shifting sand, put you in touch with some of your deepest dreams and desires. In the wake of the relationship, you will feel grief, not for the loss of the relationship but for the loss of the mirage of the relationship that you took as reality. What you need to remember is that your girlfriend built that mirage from material you provided. In recovery, distill from those dreams the truth of your own best vision for your life. Begin to cherish that truth. Begin to trust that you can move toward that vision on your own. Peace, the author of *Psychopath Free: Recovering from Emotionally Abusive Relationships with Narcissists, Sociopaths, and Other Toxic People* (2013) offers this vision of recovery:

> It will open your eyes to human nature, our broken society, and perhaps most important of all: your own spirit. It's a dark journey that will throw you into spells of depression, rage, and loneliness. It will unravel your deepest insecurities, leaving you with a lingering emptiness that haunts your every breath. But ultimately, it will heal you. You will become stronger than you could ever imagine. You will understand who you are truly meant to be. And in the end, you will be glad it happened. Kindle Edition, p.1

Many of my clients who are in the early stages of leaving a relationship with a personality disordered partner worry that they will never have the energy, time, or trust to open their hearts to another relationship. They worry about a new sense of hyper-vigilance, and struggle with the disorientation that follows the realization that they fell in love with someone who purposefully betrayed them. They wonder if they will be able to screen out in the future women who have the potential to bring similar kinds of trouble into their lives.

If you experience some of this kind of worry, pessimism, and doubt, know that it is simply part of the process of grieving, integrating the experience, and preparing for what comes next. Over and over, with the passage of time, making sense of the experience, and the cultivation of a deeper relationship with one's own experience, intuition, and judgment, women do move on from toxic relationships and into healthy partnerships. Knowing what you know now, you will be better at listening to the warning signals, better at taking things slowly, better at drawing boundaries, and better at cultivating relationships founded in kindness, respect, and mutuality. The process can't be rushed, but it will unfold in its own way as you do the work of recovering. Peace, who founded an on-line support forum at psychopathfree.com, puts it eloquently:

> Once you're able to trust fully, your physical and emotional intimacy will blossom like a flower— growing and maturing from the past. You're finally able to apply all the things you've been learning throughout the healing process. You know what you deserve, and you know who you are. You are able to freely give your loving energy because it's respected & cherished, instead of being wasted on a black hole. With psychopaths, you never know where you stand. You live in a constant state of uncertainty, wondering each day whether or not they care about you. Your entire life is consumed by this day-by-day struggle. But with real love, all of this garbage is forgotten. You do not question yourself. It is a mutual partnership of dedication and passion. 2013, p. 140

You are capable of partnerships infused with mutual interest, shared excitement, and reciprocal support. As you heal from this toxic relationship, trust that there will come a day when you are ready to connect again, and a person with whom a real connection is possible. Each day you move further away from your toxic relationship, each day you honor yourself more deeply, is a day that you create a little more of the happiness, tranquility, and security that you deserve.

BECOME A FIERCE STEWARD OF YOUR LIFE, WELL-BEING, & HAPPINESS

In the course of this short book, we have taken a look at the dramatic personality disorders and how they interfere with relationships. We have considered how your relationship with your girlfriend in particular may be thwarted by the presence of a personality disorder and the difficult behaviors associated with it. We've explored some special challenges lesbians face in partner selection, and how these may make us vulnerable to starting or persisting in relationships with women who have personality disorders. Our concerns about homophobia, heterosexism, and airing the community's dirty laundry may also impede our willingness to risk asking for help or guidance in difficult relationships, leading us to suffer in silence.

Your first attraction to this book may have been from an interest in learning more about how narcissistic, sociopathic, and borderline personality disorders may explain the unsatisfying, confusing, hurtful, and demoralizing patterns of interaction in your relationship. I hope this book has been helpful in that regard. Beyond your first impulse, I believe you sought out a book like this because you know in your heart and in your head that you deserve to be in a relationship in which you feel valued, loved, supported, and inspired, one in which you receive kindness, reciprocity, and mutuality and experience joy, fun, and delight with a woman you trust, admire, and respect. My hope is that you will feel yourself encouraged here that you can have that kind of relationship, even if you cannot have it with the most recent woman in your life. The first step in that direction is making yourself free, available, and committed to having the kind of life that will bring you lasting joy.

Getting Free from Crazy-Making Relationships